Counterrevolution and Repression in the Politics of Education

W0006740

MW0\1o6\00

Counterrevolution and Repression in the Politics of Education

At the Midnight of Dissent

Sean Noah Walsh

LEXINGTON BOOKS
Lanham • Boulder • New York • Toronto • Plymouth, UK

Published by Lexington Books
A wholly owned subsidiary of Rowman & Littlefield
4501 Forbes Boulevard, Suite 200, Lanham, Maryland 20706
www.rowman.com

10 Thornbury Road, Plymouth PL6 7PP, United Kingdom

Copyright © 2014 by Lexington Books

All rights reserved. No part of this book may be reproduced in any form or by any
electronic or mechanical means, including information storage and retrieval systems,
without written permission from the publisher, except by a reviewer who may quote
passages in a review.

British Library Cataloguing in Publication Information Available

Library of Congress Cataloging-in-Publication Data

Library of Congress Cataloging-in-Publication Data Available

ISBN 978-0-7391-8672-5 (cloth : alk. paper) — ISBN 978-0-7391-8673-2 (electronic)

♾™ The paper used in this publication meets the minimum requirements of American
National Standard for Information Sciences Permanence of Paper for Printed Library
Materials, ANSI/NISO Z39.48-1992.

Printed in the United States of America

To the memory of Dwight C. Kiel.

Contents

Acknowledgments

I am deeply grateful to the friends and colleagues who expended their own valuable time in helping me think through and improve this project. When I consider what this book represents, the greatest debt is undoubtedly owed to Ron Cox. His encouragement and patience as he listened to me fumble through crude iterations and arguments was extraordinary. Despite having an enormous set of his own responsibilities, I have never known Ron to turn me away. Moreover, he persistently reminded me that political theory, aside from its disciplinary demands, is about what *ought* to be and that none of us are served terribly well in the long view by timidity and safe bets. A serious debt is also owed to my teaching assistant, Bryant Sculos, who went well beyond any reasonable set of duties or obligations by reading early versions of the manuscripts providing sharp insights on a number of important points, and serving as another source of encouragement. Clem Fatovic and Harry Gould helped me immeasurably in getting this project off the ground. They read the initial outline for the book, formed after a summer afternoon of idle musing. When this project was at its most fragile stage, when it could have easily been crushed and discarded by a dismissive, hasty reading, Clem and Harry offered the validation and confidence I needed to proceed. Brian Nelson, who I will forever affectionately refer to as "cranky old man reviewer," was greatly helpful in reading the manuscript and sharing his own experiences from the leftism of the sixties and seventies. At various stages, I also received very helpful counsel from John Clark, Matthew Caverly, and Ty Solomon. I owe further gratitude to Thomas Biebricher for first introducing me to the works of Herbert Marcuse, and to Les Thiele for imparting the precept that how we write is no less important than what we write. Finally, I owe, as always, tremendous appreciation to my wife, Suzi, for her unyielding support and tolerance with my late-night writing sessions, endless rants, and any other impositions that I have callously forgotten. Finally, I would be remiss if I did not thank the anonymous reviewers supplied by Lexington Books, and the editorial staff, especially Justin Race and Alissa Parra for their support in the concluding stages of the project.

Chapter One

On the Obsolescence of Critical Theory

No battlefield becomes the site of carnage without the ideology that first makes it permissible to spill blood. No shot is fired, rifle aimed, or cartridge loaded without the political framework that validates those actions beforehand. These axioms are already familiar to the readers of critical theory and neo-Marxism. In those traditions, ideology became an important object of examination as the hope for an authentic revolution to upend capitalism came to naught. Following the First World War, when workingmen from all countries enthusiastically passed on the chance to embrace solidarity and united only in mutual slaughter, it became clear that capitalism perpetuated itself through more than its productive forces. Ideology, as Louis Althusser noted, facilitates the preservation of the very relationships through which production occurs. Still, it is one matter to consider how capitalism reproduces itself, as Althusser does. It is another to ask how the forces and agents of capitalism work in the realm of ideology to prevent threats before they can even begin to arise.

This project examines the ideological aspects of the counterrevolution underway in late capitalism. By counterrevolution, I refer to the historical conditions identified by the critical theorist and Marxist philosopher Herbert Marcuse, which he discussed for the most part in his later writings. Counterrevolution, at this moment, pertains to those forces and practices arrayed in opposition to the possibility of revolution and in defense of capitalism. I contend that these practices have quietly permeated the politics of reason, especially in the institutions of education. It did not declare itself as counterrevolution upon its arrival in the school. Its agents may not even recognize themselves under this mantle. Counterrevolution denotes more than a struggle between ideologies. Rather, in the thought of Herbert Marcuse, it indicates the historical effort by capitalism and its agents to prevent the viability or advancement of utopianism, which is nothing more than the ensemble of dissenting and critical projects that aim at imagining a world beyond capitalism.

The ideas of Herbert Marcuse received considerable and deserved attention during the 1960s and 1970s, the time when he was widely considered to be the intellectual conscience of the New Left. In fact, Marcuse gained a degree of notoriety and was the object of occasional death threats for his support of the radical student movement, a position that distinguished him from other critical theorists such as Max Horkheimer and Theodor Adorno. However, the present moment appears to reflect a diminished interest in Marcuse, most unfortunately among political theorists and political philosophers. There had been a period of great interest in Marcuse, yet as Stanley Aronowitz (1999, 133) laments, "it seems that he had just fifteen minutes of fame; his work is now out of fashion and virtually unread by students, activists and academics, save for the narrow circle of those who work and teach in the tradition of the Critical Theory of the Frankfurt School." This may be owed, in part, to the perception of Marcuse as an essentialist thinker at a moment when the various forms of anti-essentialism command considerably greater attention. Fuchs (2001, 30–31), for example, identifies Marcuse, and all critical theory following in the Hegelian tradition, as subscribing to an excessively broad concept of ideology, constituting "anything that perpetuates and justifies the status quo as the inevitable outcome of technical efficiency and instrumental rationality." Or, there is Ernesto Laclau and Chantal Mouffe's (1985, 87) criticism that Marcuse situates the working class—to the exclusion of others—as the central subject of emancipation. Accordingly, they find that his commentary on the production of an ideologically incapacitated subject, the infamous one-dimensional man, has been unfounded (ibid. 161). Beyond this type of claim, Marcuse's critics have often based their arguments on distorted premises and even blatantly ad hominem attacks. Alasdair MacIntyre (1970, 14) claims that Marcuse "seldom if ever, gives us any reason to believe that what he is writing is true." While MacIntyre is correct that his works do not rely on empirical data, Marcuse does give us reasons in support of his various theses. Strictly speaking, the same assessment could easily be made of MacIntyre's (1984, 22) interesting but largely unsubstantiated assertion of a purportedly lost moral grammar enjoyed by the ancients. His work provides the reader with no evidence that a fuller vision of morality ever existed. Nevertheless, MacIntyre does take Marcuse's ideas into serious consideration, and his criticism merits careful reading. Different is Allan Bloom's (1987, 226) description of Marcuse as nothing more than an author of "trashy culture criticism with a heavy sex interest." Given Bloom's clearly conservative views, his opposition to Marcuse is not terribly surprising. However, he musters no serious engagement with Marcuse's work, only a casual dismissal that goes unsubstantiated. Indeed, Stephen Eric Bronner

(2002, 124) rebuts the idea that Marcuse was some sort of literary libertine, suggesting that he was instead "a moralist par excellence" whose "thinking had no place for sexual promiscuity, drugs, rock and roll, or pornography." Even more bizarrely, Eliseo Vivas (1971, 10) contends that Marcuse, had he acquired the power to do so, "would out-Robespierre Robespierre, out–Saint Just Saint Just, and do better than Stalin and Hitler rolled into one." Given that Marcuse never called for, or even implied, favor in the enactment of purges and terror, openly detested Stalinism, and in fact explicitly rejected state violence, Vivas's claim is patently wrong.

My aim here is not to defend Marcuse against MacIntyre's contention that his arguments lack evidence, Bloom's allegation of salaciousness, Vivas's rather strange conjecture, or even the portrayals of essentialism. In the first place, Douglas Kellner (2004, 82) has already argued quite effectively that Marcuse, in fact, "anticipates the post-structuralist critique of the subject." That is, according to Kellner's arguments, Marcuse can only be tenuously labeled an essentialist. Second, neglecting a thinker like Marcuse, or deriding his character as substitute for contending with his arguments, is really to our detriment. The pertinence of his political views, especially in the present condition of capitalism, far outweighs any problems that follow from his metaphysics. In comparison to the political insights he offers, any purported essentialism is of ancillary import. Claims that he is a writer of sleaze or a frustrated genocidal tyrant genuinely lack merit and are thoroughly contradicted by a body of work that consistently stakes claims of exactly the opposite nature. Marcuse warns us of the creeping counterrevolution, and we ignore him at our own peril.

Even among those scholars who have amenably investigated Marcuse's ideas, the issue of counterrevolution has been afforded very little examination, remaining a largely peripheral concern. Most recently, Farr (2009, 178) demonstrates how the consequences of a one-dimensional society leave the promise of American democracy, which Marcuse approved in its idealized form, an as-yet unfulfilled project. In various instances, Bronner (1994; 2002; 2011) makes extensive use of Marcuse's work in mapping possible routes for radical politics to resist the contemporaneous tendency toward conservatism, though counterrevolution remains a largely background issue. By making the subject of counterrevolution a direct focus, this project supports that aim. Kellner (1994, 260) directly ponders the utility of Marcuse's views on counterrevolution as they might pertain to ecology, but his primary concerns are focused elsewhere. For her part, Steuernagel (1994, 90) demonstrates how his disappointment over the success of counterrevolution, and the subsequent disenchantment with the working and middle class, led Marcuse toward a more serious engagement with gender and feminism. Lind (1985, 211) situates *Counterrevolution and Revolt* as an important aspect of Marcuse's later works, especially its claims on the importance of rationality in facilitating revolution. Here as well, the issue of counterrevolution itself remains largely unexamined. The same is basically true in the intellectual biographies constructed by Fry (1974), Katz (1982), and Martineau (1986). Furthermore, of those scholarly projects that have examined his views on education, none bring the framework of counterrevolution to the forefront.

There is a notable dearth of attention to this subject, which Marcuse felt was important enough that he dedicated his penultimate text, *Counterrevolution & Revolt* to it. This paucity may be in part due to the fact that Marcuse never systematically situated his observations on counterrevolution within the constellation of his larger body of work, something that I hope to advance in the concluding chapter. Still, in the context of current economic crises, globalization, and the apparent ideological hardening of capitalism in the West, it is time that Marcuse's views on counterrevolution received serious attention. My aims with this project include precisely that. First, I wish to recover and amplify Marcuse's observations on this important subject. Second, I deploy his observations on counterrevolution as a framework for interpreting certain exertions of power in the politics of reason. By "politics of reason," I refer to the various contestations in the present moment over the acquisition, representation, and exercise of reason, especially as it pertains to the criticism of, and dissent against, capitalism. More specifically, I use this framework to examine how the manipulation of the academic curriculum, the representation of intellectuals, the production of students as ideological subjects, and the emphasis on so-called online teaching serves counterrevolutionary aims.

Herbert Marcuse was born in July 1898 to a middle-class Jewish family in Berlin. The Marcuse family was largely secular, and apparently identified first as Germans, than as Jews. Marcuse was drafted into the German army in 1916, but his poor eyesight probably saved his life as it prevented him from serving at the frontlines. Because of his logistical, rear-echelon role, in the military, Marcuse became increasingly politicized, witnessing desperate circumstances that plagued the country including "food riots, strikes, profiteering, and general unrest" (MacKey 2001). These events pushed him further toward the political left. After the war, he studied first at Humboldt University, where he associated with Walter Benjamin and Georg Lukacs. It was at the University of Freiburg where Marcuse came under the direction of the phenomenologist Edmund Husserl and his protégé, Martin Heidegger (Martineau 1986, 10). Although Marcuse hoped to finish his studies under Heidegger's supervision, the rise of Nazism, and Heidegger's decision to join the Nazi party, effectively eliminated that aspiration. Rather than persist under increasingly hostile circumstances, Marcuse emigrated to the United States via Switzerland in 1934. After a series of conversations and interviews with Friedrich Pollock, Marcuse was invited to join the Institute for Social Research (Katz 1982, 86). Along with other members of the Institute who had fled Germany, such as Max Horkheimer and Theodor Adorno, Marcuse helped establish the foundation of what would become known as the Frankfurt School of Critical Theory from their base at Columbia University. During the Second World War, he took a position as senior intelligence analyst with the Office of Strategic Services, precursor to the Central Intelligence Agency (Marks 1970, 9). In fact, Marcuse's government service, which would seem particularly odd given his political leanings, lasted until 1951 when the anticommunist fervor of Joseph McCarthy made government employment inhospitable for a Marxist. After his time at the OSS concluded, Marcuse's academic career began in earnest. From 1951 until 1954, he was employed by Columbia, and then began work at Brandeis University. During the 1960s he became a more vocal supporter of dissidents, student protestors, and radical political movements. When Brandeis allowed his contract to expire, Marcuse joined the faculty at the University of California at San Diego, where he continued his support of radical politics. It was during this later period that he became the object of intense controversy. Newspapers in San Diego, along with the local chapter of the American Legion, campaigned for his removal from the university. He received (grammatically incorrect) death threats attributed to the Ku Klux Klan and was also, apparently, the object of repudiating remarks by Pope Paul VI (Marks 1970, 7 and MacKey 2001).

This project focuses on a specific aspect of Marcuse's later work, counterrevolution, employing it as a framework to assess the conditions under which the uses of reason for the purposes of dissent have been subverted. Marcuse approached this subject as a historical matter. My aim is to examine certain phenomena within the politics of reason, which are most acutely expressed through the exertion of power in the areas of education, through the perspective of this historical condition. How are the representation, acquisition, and exercise of reason shaped by the counterrevolution in late capitalism? How has counterrevolution manifested itself ideologically at the scene of education, particularly within the school? By approaching them from the standpoint of counterrevolution, seemingly disparate practices can be argued to share the unified aim of thwarting utopianism, the critical gestures that seek to advance genuinely alternative political futures. That is, by neutralizing the instruments of criticism in advance, alienating reason through the representation of intellectuals as inhuman, reproducing the relations of consumption, and narrowing the aesthetic dimension of teaching, the counterrevolution works through ideology to represent dissent as the paramount political obscenity.

Why should we consider these phenomena as part of a counterrevolutionary strategy, or, asked differently, why is the framework of counterrevolution important in examining these issues? By deploying Marcuse's observations on counterrevolution, we are better able to observe the systematic subversion of reason and recognize that these are not isolated tactics but those belonging to a unified strategy. By viewing these issues through the historical framework of counterrevolution, we can understand that all of these phenomena bear a common aim—the preventative suppression of the utopian. Thinking these issues through, Marcuse's idea on counterrevolution permits us to recognize that seemingly fragmentary, unconnected tactics actually belong to a singular anti-utopian strategy. As such, counterrevolution ought to be understood as a set of tactics working toward the subversion of reason, preemptively neutralizing the intellectual conditions that may promote revolutionary consciousness in the future. According to the premises of historical materialism, counterrevolution is expressed differently according to the mode of production in which it is situated. This counterrevolution, the one that Marcuse draws our attention to, is no different in that regard, using the available materials to manipulate the politics of reason.

In the course of these analyses, I attempt to bring Marcuse's views together with a number of other thinkers, such as Louis Althusser (chapter 2), Algirdas Julien Greimas (chapter 3), Georg Lukacs (chapter 4), Walter Benjamin (chapter 5), and Fredric Jameson (chapter 6). In the third chapter, I will employ the views of the structuralist semiologist A. J. Greimas to further our understanding of the counterrevolution that is ongoing. Likewise, I repeatedly return to Althusser's views on ideology and aesthetics. While it may be my own naivety, I see no reason why structuralist and humanist Marxisms cannot be made to share the same space. Territorial divisiveness is counterproductive, and more likely the result of disciplinary and occupational demands that effectively partition solidarity in Marxist thought than the consequence of genuine incompatibility. After all, if our visions of Marx can accommodate both structuralism and humanism, then those two variants of his tradition ought to have something to say to one another.

Chapter 2 reconsiders what might be misconstrued as attacks by the state on its own institutions of education as efforts, hidden under the false necessity of budgetary crises, to nullify the conditions for dissent before they can develop. I examine Louis Althusser's theory of ideology in light of recent events in education policy and practice. Althusser details the crucial role of ideology in reproducing the relations of production. Material forces alone do not dictate social structures. It is ideology that conditions how individuals relate to materials, institutions, and other individuals. Althusser explains that the dispensation of ideology is the function of what he calls the "Ideological State Apparatus." The most important aspect of the Ideological State Apparatus, and, therefore, the most important source of ideology and reproducing the relations of production in late capitalism, is the school. If Althusser is correct with regards to the crucial role played by the school in dispensing ideology and perpetuating the capitalist mode of production, then we should not expect to observe policies that undermine the school by defunding it or excessively taxing its resources. Yet, that is apparently what we find in the present: state governments run by the most ardent supporters of capitalism sapping universities and public schools of funds. How can we account for this apparent gap in Althusser's theory? Here I apply Marcuse's concept of counterrevolution to demonstrate that in the context of economic crisis, the state acts on behalf of capitalism to weaken the possibilities for revolutionary consciousness before they can develop. Rather than weakening the school, the state uses its material power to redirect resources and enforce a technical curriculum that reduces the potency of the intellectual faculties and preemptively aborts the development of critical sensibilities

Chapter 3 examines the structure of anti-intellectualism, with particular attention paid to the role of "the professor." There, I examine the condition of anti-intellectual discourse in late capitalism. Curiously, some of the most virulent attacks on intellectuals originate with other intellectuals. Academics such as Mark Lilla, Thomas Sowell, Raymond Aron, and others have published lengthy monographs on the allegedly pernicious effects intellectuals inflict upon society. Outside academic circles, politicians frequently voice their disdain and distrust for intellectuals, oftentimes with a special invective directed toward academics. "Professor" is seemingly a designation of special opprobrium within anti-intellectual discourse. How, then, does the representation of intellectuals serve counterrevolutionary aims? In this chapter, I combine the insights of the structuralist semiologist A. J. Greimas, along with those of Marcuse and Jameson to analyze the rhetoric of anti-intellectual discourse. For the most part, derogatory rhetoric against intellectuals is expressed as one of two terms in a binary of potency. That is to say, intellectuals are represented as either dangerously powerful or perversely impotent. As I will demonstrate, both images are unified by the representation of the intellectual as inhuman. In this fashion, reason is defamed by first defaming the purveyors of reason.

Chapter 4 documents the ascendancy of a new dynamic in the development of college and university students. Rather than purely cultivate students-as-workers, the emphasis is now placed on developing students-as-consumers. It has been frequently noted that capitalism displays a remarkable adaptability. Counterrevolution remains an important component of this capacity for preservation. In this chapter, I will consider how counterrevolution has served to ameliorate some of the contradictions inherent to capitalism, in particular by addressing the ideological development of students in higher education. Marx tells us that capitalism creates its own gravediggers by creating an alienated class of workers. Historically, schools produced these workers. By the beginning of the twentieth century, members of the proletariat were being supplied with a rudimentary education in primary schools while higher-ranking functionaries received their credentials in the universities. Now, if we examine the scene of the modern university, or the school in general, the emphasis appears to have shifted. The focus no longer pertains to the production of workers. While that remains to some degree, the emphasis is instead on the production of consumers. Moreover, I argue this shift bears the clear counterrevolutionary aim of resolving the contradiction of the proletariat. Creating workers is tantamount to creating a potential army of revolutionaries because the collective experience of work can facilitate class consciousness. Developing students into consumers negates this possibility because of the wholly individualist experience of consumption.

Chapter 5 addresses the effects of the increasingly frequent directives toward online teaching. Marcuse asserts that art maintains a revolutionary promise located in its ability to generate thought-provoking novelties. Different forms raise the space for inspiring new kinds of thinking. Here, I draw on Althusser's aesthetic theory in order to justify teaching as harboring an artistic dimension. In that regard, teaching is a structural effect of both art and science. The emphasis toward mandating online technology imposes a highly limited aesthetic on teaching, thus suffocating its capacity for provoking different kinds of thinking. I argue, therefore, that the expanding trend of online teaching serves counterrevolutionary aims by limiting the possible range of aesthetic forms, robbing teaching of its artistic dimension, and leaving only a sterile science behind.

Chapter 6 situates Marcuse's views on counterrevolution within the larger body of his ideas, and bridges his work with that of Fredric Jameson's. Rather than being understood as an extraneous appendix compared to his more celebrated ideas, counterrevolution is integral in understanding how the concepts of surplus-repression and the one-dimensional subject function together in this age. As I demonstrate, the subversion of reason caused by the various tactics of counterrevolution create a "repressive conduit" in which the faculties of imagination are drawn away from the subject inhabiting late capitalism. The effect is to increase the scope of what Jameson calls "the political unconscious," narrowing the imagination of a one-dimensional subject who increasingly accepts utopianism as the paramount political obscenity. I conclude with a modest call for resistance by educators and students against these efforts.

A return to Marcuse and his observations on counterrevolution has become vital. At a time of economic turmoil in which the middle and working classes are made to suffer for the follies of the powerful, and often become the zealous advocates of so-called austerity measures, the ideas of a thinker such as Marcuse, which are both radical and grounded in day-to-day life, are sorely needed. However, if a return to Marcuse is in order, the question remains as to how that return ought to be conducted. As best we can, I suggest we ought to embrace Marcuse as he intended and avoid the tendency to sanitize, rewrite, or reconstruct his views according to our present sensibilities. Of course, the possibility for accessing the unmediated truth of any author is confronted with considerable difficulty. As Roland Barthes (1977, 148) reminds us, reading becomes its own form of inscription. That being said, there is a difference between recognizing the barriers obstructing the noumenal truth of an author and deliberately mutilating his or her works according to the fleeting sensibilities of the moment. Marcuse may seem dated. The notion that there are actually elites who consciously wield power toward the ends of domination might appear archaic and passé. Such a vision, which belonged to the ethos of the Frankfurt School in its early iterations, has become eschewed in favor of more recent views lamenting how we are all more or less subjects of a mutually constituted power. The idea that there may be puppeteers who reap the profits of exploitation is thought embarrassingly crude. While political theory may have moved on from the early Frankfurt School, the original critical theorists—Lukacs, Horkheimer, Adorno, Benjamin, Fromm, and especially Marcuse—have much to teach us provided we avoid the condescending gesture of trying to rehabilitate them according to our most fashionable sensibilities. After all, Aronowitz (1999, 135) notes that while many of their acolytes abandoned "all possible master discourses, especially Marxism," later theorists such as Jacques Derrida and Gilles Deleuze had actually returned to Marx and Marxism toward the end of their careers. Likewise, Michel Foucault admitted that, had he been aware of the Frankfurt School earlier, he "would not have said a certain amount of nonsense" (Aronowitz, ibid.). Social and political theory has much more to do with art than science. Political theory does not become obsolete, only unfashionable, which is far more an indictment against the conceit of the present than those ideas belonging to theorists of the past. In the final analysis, Marcuse does not need our help; we need his.

Chapter Two

Abortion of the Intellect

Counterrevolution in the Politics of Curriculum

THE PHILOSOPHY OF CORRUPTION

With its various apologies, Western political philosophy essentially begins by defending itself, even if halfheartedly, against the charges that it embodies a pernicious influence, a corruptor of the youth. Yet, according to the structuralist-Marxist thinker Louis Althusser, that is precisely the world-historical purpose of philosophy; in its truest form it serves no function other than revolutionary, anti-bourgeois, and radical aims. As Althusser notes, "philosophy represents the people's class struggle in theory" (Althusser 2001a, 8). There are, of course, conservative and bourgeois examples of philosophy, but, insofar as it harbors revolutionary aims, philosophy is indeed corruption, the corruption of those very same conservative and bourgeois values, as well as the domination that follows. Throughout its history, philosophy has been "a perpetual war of ideas" reflecting different class positions (Althusser 1990b, 255). In Althusser's view, Karl Marx inaugurated a profound transformation by "putting philosophy into practice in a new and disconcerting form" (ibid., 265). In that sense, authentic philosophy is an instrument of *dissent*. Accordingly, he describes philosophy as a means "to hasten the end of bourgeois ideological hegemony" (ibid., 264).

Under this view, if philosophy is meant to raise consciousness and develop routes of criticism and dissent, then the school, as the supreme ideological institution of modern education, serves exactly the opposite purpose. The school, in capitalism, stands in opposition to philosophy, at least philosophy in its revolutionary variant. In the present era, the state maintains authority over a vast network of educational institutions, from public schools to uni-

11

versities. In the United States, even private schools are subject to accreditation agencies that receive their final validation from the Secretary of Education. Instead of serving the philosophic aim of cultivating critical reason, the school—in capitalism—is meant to convert the individual into a subject of the prevailing, dominant, and, therefore, capitalist ideology. That is, in Althusser's view, there is no greater, more useful, and effective appendage for the dispensation of ideology than the school. In Althusserian theory, the school serves an absolutely vital function in the perpetuation of capitalism (Althusser 2001b, 106).

Despite this essentially conservative role, the school has seemingly become the object of deliberate debilitation. These assaults were not launched, however, by leftist critics discontented with the perpetuation of capitalist ideology. Instead, various measures stressing and burdening the school have originated from among the staunchest supporters of capitalism, some of the most conservative elements originating within *the state itself.* That is, under the most reliably capitalist administrators, the resources for secondary and higher education have been destabilized. Indicative of this trend, following his inauguration Governor Rick Scott, Republican from the state of Florida, unveiled a series of severe budget reductions for the state's public universities and public schools. [1] Additional resources, under the governor's plan, have been reallocated away from the arts, social sciences, and humanities and toward programs in science, technology, and engineering (or otherwise indicated by the acronym "STEM"). [2] Of course, one might argue that these budget reductions and reallocations merely represent a pragmatic response to the general economic crisis and significant revenue losses that followed. Florida, after all, has no income tax, instead relying heavily on property taxes. Much of this revenue evaporated after 2008 as a result of the massive contraction in the housing market. [3]

That explanation is inadequate. As demonstrated by the historic reactions to heterodox thinking, some elements of what Herbert Marcuse called "the Establishment" have tended, long before any economic crisis, to target education in both content and resources. Marcuse (1972b, p. 27) was particularly concerned over the "systematic restrictions on the humanities and social sciences, where traditionally non-conformist education has found a niche." Of particular concern was that such restrictions were thinly veiled efforts to convert schools and universities into clients of industry, turning out future workers for "the established society" (ibid., p. 28). Education remains a perennially contested object of power. Althusser observes "what thus seems to take place outside ideology (to be precise, in the streets), in reality takes place in ideology" (Althusser 2001b, 118). Policy actions garbed in the language of "necessity" are often the most ideological. In that regard, while the economic crisis may have precipitated action on the part of the state, that is entirely different than the crisis necessitating the peculiar manifestation of that action. The reallocations of funding, and redirection of students—toward science, technology, and engineering and away from social sciences, arts, and humanities—cannot be attributed to a budget problem. None of that was necessitated by economic conditions. Instead, the economic crisis served as an opportunity to manipulate the curriculum and preventatively dismantle the means of dissent from emerging within the institutions of education.

The question becomes as to how these apparent trends in education policy can be understood according to the premises of late Marxism. If Althusser is correct about the crucial role of the school in the dispensation of capitalist ideology, then the expansion of education resources, especially under an unapologetically corporate administrator, would be expected. Indeed, even if a budget crisis compelled extraordinary measures, then education ought to be among the last areas one would expect to find spending decreases. After all, a crisis would only heighten the need for more intensive ideological dissemination. Even the social sciences and the humanities, which, according to Althusser, have always represented petty bourgeoisie ideology, ought to be preserved if not enlarged in order to further the ends of capitalism (Althusser 2001a, 2). Instead, we find just the opposite. The school in general, and the social sciences, arts, and humanities in particular, have become subject to policies of diminution.

How can this apparent contradiction be reconciled? More importantly, how can we understand the effect of this strategy, and related actions in education? One answer might be to conclude that Althusser is wrong, that his observations on the centrality of the school to the ideological perpetuation of capitalism are simply incorrect. My argument, however, is that this curiosity does not demonstrate an error with Althusserian theory, only a gap originating from his focus on structure. I suggest that this gap can be accounted for by situating these policies within the context of Herbert Marcuse's humanist Marxism.[4] Indeed, Marcuse explains that we inhabit the period of an ongoing counterrevolution in late capitalism. Under the effects of this historical condition, reason is increasingly subjected to narrower and narrower horizons. As Marcuse warns:

> Thus emerges a pattern of one-dimensional thought and behavior in which ideas, aspirations, and objectives that, by their content, transcend the established universe of discourse and action are either repelled or reduced to terms of this universe. They are redefined by the rationality of the given system and of its quantitative extension. (Marcuse 1964, p. 12)

That which does not conform to the parameters of late capitalism is dismissed, excluded, or appropriated and repackaged to become safely exploitable. The school, broadly construed, is instrumental in achieving these conversions.

Applied to the environs of the university, the term "counterrevolution" might appear incongruous. After all, counterrevolution is probably most familiar to us in the all-too-frequent guises of bloodstained battlefields, ditches filled with the shattered corpses of dissidents, and the eerie traces of the Disappeared. Those are the clearest images of violent counterrevolution. Nevertheless, as Marcuse warns, there are other forms at work. If they are less violent, these forms are the all the more insidious precisely because they are less detectable. The success of these ideological forms is dependent on their ability to pass themselves off as something, *anything*, other than counterrevolution. Certain policies and actions serve the end of perpetuating and deepening the domain of capitalism by shaping reason. By exercising control over the representation, acquisition, and exercise of reason, the counterrevolution in late capitalism forecloses the imagination of alternative possibilities to that system. The scene of the school is where the counterrevolution is waged ideologically.

Viewed, therefore, through this perspective of the counterrevolution, the reduction and reallocation of resources are not attacks on the ideologically disposed nature of education. Rather, those actions represent an effort to reshape the curriculum in a manner that is consistent with counterrevolutionary aims. By redirecting its resources, and thereby ideologically reorienting the curriculum, the state attempts to foreclose the possibility of a revolutionary consciousness before it can even form, effectively committing an intellectual abortion that serves the aims of counterrevolution.

In the next section, I will detail the nature of Louis Althusser's theory of ideology and its relation to the institutions of education. In the third section, I offer an account of the state strategy to reorient the curriculum. With the financial and budgetary issues as a pretext, the state—under the stewardship of ardent capitalists—is explicitly steering education toward the production of ideological subjects who are more readily commodifiable and exploitable while, simultaneously, depoliticizing those same subjects. If the aim of political education, according to Lenin—an indispensible thinker for Althusser— was to demonstrate the ubiquity of politics, the state's education strategy appears to favor a policy of political neutralization, education that depoliticizes and mystifies. The fourth section situates this strategy within the context of Marcuse's observations on counterrevolution, depicting the consequences of these policies as a preventative effort to cancel the development of revolutionary consciousness, an abortion of the intellect.

HORROR BUSINESS

The origins of Althusser's theories on ideology and the state are heavily influenced by the writings of Vladimir Ilyich Lenin. Whereas Karl Marx recognized the significance of ideological forces such as religion in directing the minds of the proletariat, he suggests that the deteriorating conditions of capitalism would, on their own, expose the lies of "so many bourgeois prejudices, behind which lurk in ambush just as many bourgeois interests" (Marx 1985, p. 92). Increasingly expansive poverty would more or less shock the worker out of the need for religion. And while Marx (ibid., p. 100) acknowledged that "social conditions" and "society" intervene and control the institutions of education, it was Lenin who recognizes the efforts of the state to retard the intellectual development of revolutionary awareness.

Lenin laments that early Russian socialists adopted such naïve and reckless approaches to conducting their work, especially with regard to secrecy, that government raids met with great ease. Revolutionary cells were neutralized with such success "that the masses of the workers literally lost all their leaders" (Lenin 1987, p. 129). The state attacked its adversaries intellectually and theoretically in order to thwart the spread of seditious ideas. In response, for Lenin, the imperative was placed on promulgating what he called "political education." As Lenin notes:

> The consciousness of the masses of the workers cannot be genuine class consciousness, unless the workers learn to observe from concrete, and above all from topical, political facts and events, *every* other social class and *all* the manifestations of the intellectual, ethical and political life of these classes; unless they learn to apply practically the materialist analyses and the materialist estimate of *all* aspects of the life and activity of *all* classes, strata and groups of the population. (Lenin 1987, p. 104)

Deprived of revolutionary intellectuals, the working class could only be exposed to bourgeois, or reformist as opposed to revolutionary, values and interpretations. The aim of Leninist political education is to expose the abuses inherent to capitalism by representing world-historical events within the context of class struggle. It is, therefore, the role of the vanguard to wrest the depiction of events, such as a strike or a riot, away from the bourgeois explanation that workers are merely lashing out as a result of being lazy, ungrateful, and savage, instead demonstrating how such matters result from exploitation. The same holds true for Marcuse (1972b, p. 47), who writes, "All authentic education is political education." By this, Marcuse means that, insofar as an activity can be said to raise a critical consciousness, it can be called "education."

Drawing upon these Leninist insights, Althusser more closely examines the means by which the state resists revolutionary political education. Society is more than an assortment of technological and material forces. Those are, in Marxist theory, the means of production. Without specified relations of production, there is no necessary use for any set of materials. That a factory exists does not necessitate a particular organization or use. It is the relations of production coupled with the means of production that amount to a historically given mode of production. Essentially, the relations of production are the political organization for the mode of production, and, since the relations of production do not necessarily follow from any given material element, Althusser's investigation begins by questioning how it is that the relations of production are themselves reproduced. As he notes, "I shall say that the reproduction of labor power requires not only a reproduction of skills, but also, at the same time, a reproduction of its submission to the rules of the established order" (Althusser 2001b, p. 89). That is, he asks what are the conditions under which social order itself is re-created.

The state assumes a central role in this task, and its efforts are divided between two important mechanisms: the Repressive State Apparatus (RSA) and the Ideological State Apparatus (ISA). Briefly, the Repressive State Apparatus is responsible for using force to secure and maintain control of the means of production. Included within this apparatus are the various agencies of martial force: the police, the military, strikebreakers, prisons, etc. As Althusser (2001b, 96) explains, "Repressive suggests that the State Apparatus in question 'functions by violence.'" It is the role of the Repressive State Apparatus to suppress, by violent means, any revolutionary action or any action that would disrupt bourgeois control and ownership over the means of production.

If, however, the Ideological State Apparatus adequately performs its role, then the Repressive State Apparatus can remain relatively dormant. This is precisely because it is the purpose of the former to ensure that every individual is a willing participant in the reproduction of capitalism. The Ideological State Apparatus functions by means of "interpellation," the process of calling an ideological subject into being (Althusser 2001b, p. 119). Whereas the RSA primarily functions by means of violence and force, the ISA performs through the dissemination of ideology. In that sense, the ISA promotes the extant conditions of society as appropriate, right, natural, and desirable, perpetuating "the imaginary relationship of individuals to their real conditions of existence" (ibid., p. 109). It is the Ideological State Apparatus that is crucial for reproducing the relations of production and maintaining the façade of harmony and the lie of mutual benefit. Without the ISA, preserving power relations within society would fall under the aegis of the RSA and become nothing more than a matter of naked violence. At that point, the relations of production are only tenuously held together.

Althusser explains that the Ideological State Apparatus resides within the superstructure of the mode of production, meaning the nature of the ISA is determined by the material forces arrayed within the technological base of society. The primary locus of ideological indoctrination during the feudal mode of production was the Church. Religious instruction was (and remains), in the Marxist analysis, nothing more than ideology propagated under a supernatural façade. However, with the ascension of the capitalist mode of production, the Church gradually relinquished its primacy within the Ideological State Apparatus and was replaced by the school. Ideology veiled in the holy word was gradually superseded by ideology veiled in the scientific theorem. As Althusser (ibid., p. 104) states, "Nevertheless, in this concert, one ideological State apparatus certainly has the dominant role, although hardly anyone lends an ear to its music: it is so silent! This is the School." And just as religion was used to ensure a passive, pliable population, scholastic instruction now serves the aim of promoting the technical training and values necessary to reproduce the capitalist relations of production. Ideology, in Althusser's theory, creates subjects, and the school dispenses ideology. It is, therefore, the school that is most responsible for creating ideological subjects in the present mode of production. The individual is always already an ideological subject. There is no outside or beyond ideology that is accessible to the subject (ibid., p. 119). The school serves to refine, shape, and reinforce the character of ideology, to ensure acquiescence, if not outright subservience, to capitalism.

In Althusser's writings, the struggle over the ideological life of the subject is situated in education. On the one hand, philosophy bears the potential of being a revolutionary weapon insofar as it bears the promise of criticism and dissent. "Philosophy is political," he explains (Althusser 2001a, p. 1). On the other hand, the purveyors of philosophy, regardless of how they see themselves, are subjects of bourgeois ideology. Educational institutions, and especially those pertaining to higher education, are often portrayed as being a bastion of leftist sympathies. Whether or not that is the case, Althusser notes that intellectuals and academics are not revolutionaries (Althusser 2001a, p. 2). Instead, they are functionaries of the Ideological State Apparatus; they belong to the petite bourgeoisie, no matter how they might struggle to promote alternative values. Ultimately, the efforts to subvert bourgeois values in the classroom fail. As Althusser notes:

> Philosophy teachers are teachers, i.e. intellectuals employed in a given education system and subject to that system, performing, as a mass, the social function of inculcating the "values of the ruling ideology." The fact that there may be a certain amount of "play" in schools and other institutions which enables individual teachers to turn their teaching and reflection against these established "values" does not change the mass effect of the philosophical teaching function. Philosophers are intellectuals and therefore petty bourgeois, subject as a mass to bourgeois and petty-bourgeois ideology. (Althusser 2001c, p. 42)

Even the most ardent academic proponent of Marxism is only engaged in academic Marxism, teaching about a subject in a sterile environment no differently than a biology instructor might orchestrate the dissection of a frog. Regardless of how emphatically a teacher of Marxism might engage in exposing the atrocities of capitalism, it still proceeds within the safe and, more importantly, sanctioned environs of the classroom. Much like an audience at a horror movie is able to mollify itself with the occasional reminder that none of the gore was real, the class is able to dabble in the suspension of disbelief. But the most lucid sign that the state can tolerate these neutered panoramas of Marxism is that the Repressive State Apparatus remains dormant. The universities are bastions of leftist sympathies in the same manner as asylums are bastions of lunacy. Only when the divide between theory and practice is genuinely threatened is the line crossed, and the best sign of that is when the violent forces of the RSA have been activated. Thus, in Althusser's theory, it makes no difference whether or not the academy is populated with leftist sympathizers because sympathizers are not genuine revolutionaries; sympathies are not revolutions. Consequently, the academic and the intellectual are constrained to serving as unwilling (at best) vessels (or even willing vassals) of capitalist ideology.

TECHNICAL CRISIS

The explicit rationale for contracting the school apparatuses in Florida and elsewhere finds its roots in the larger global economic crisis. Although a confluence of different factors may have all contributed, the "Great Recession" was probably triggered by a precipitous collapse in the housing sector of the economy (Weisberg 2010).[5] Here as well, a variety of causes played a role in the collapse of the housing market. Financial institutions sought ever-greater profits by lending to high-risk mortgagees at elevated interest rates. Borrowers were induced and seduced into taking on debt loads they could not manage, while lenders ignored prudence in the name of profit and greed. Concurrent to these unsound transactions, speculative "house flipping" became rampant. Buyers would purchase a property solely for the purpose of then turning around in a very short timeframe to sell at a profit. House flipping, combined with the influx of new home buyers, effectively caused a rapid inflation of the housing market. Prices of new and existing homes rose dramatically.[6] Nevertheless, the lenders continued to sell homes to buyers who were clearly purchasing beyond their means. The inevitable waves of foreclosures, along with the saturation of new home construction, sparked a massive economic contraction.[7]

In the absence of any tax levied against income, the state of Florida relies largely on the revenue from sales and property taxes. Local school districts are directly funded by property taxes. When house values increased during the period of speculation and expansion, property taxes also grew. But with the multiple waves of foreclosures, and the general economic contraction that led to a massive loss of jobs, school districts lost a major source of revenue while the state also lost revenue from sales taxes as fewer jobs equated to less individual spending capacity.

According to Althusser's arguments the state should be expected to foster the enlargement of the Ideological State Apparatus, particularly in the form of the school. Regardless of deteriorating economic conditions, or perhaps especially because of that climate, it would seem imperative to retain the most crucial component of the Ideological State Apparatus. A larger and more pervasive school system would amount to more expansive ideological interpellation, and greater subscription to capitalist relations of production. This would seem all the more relevant during a time of crisis and the potential unrest that might follow. Yet, precisely the opposite appears to have happened. In Florida, we find instead policies of curtailing education spending and reallocating resources enacted by a Republican-dominated state legislature and Republican Governor Rick Scott. Indeed, prior to being elected, Scott was a career businessman and corporate chief executive officer. He explicitly campaigned on the promise to import his business experience into the management of the state and its affairs. As a candidate, Scott promised to "run government like a business" (Allen 2011). And with a decidedly conservative legislature supporting his agenda, there can be no question about the capitalist bona fides of his regime.[8]

Despite these capitalist credentials, and the Althusserian assertion that the school serves as a functionary of ruling-class ideology, the state of Florida under Rick Scott established policy that seriously stressed institutions of education. In terms of the primary and secondary institutions, the governor claimed to add $1 billion to education in 2012. However, in the previous year, he signed into law a budget that slashed education spending by $1.3 billion, thus amounting to a net loss of $300 million (DiSalvo 2012). After five consecutive years of budget reductions to the university system, the state enacted a new reduction of $300 million (Wilmath 2012a). Consequently, the University of Florida endured a 30 percent decline in its operating expenses over six years prior to the most recent budget (DiSalvo 2012). The University of Central Florida suffered a $52 million reduction in its budget, while Florida State University lost $65 million. Furthermore, when the universities requested a tuition increase to offset the budget reductions, the governor refused authorization and effectively retaliated with "a further review of the universities, with the goal of understanding 'the return on an increased investment'" (Wilmath 2012b). In effect, the universities asked for permission to seek relief and were met with an investigative reprisal.

Put into context, the public school system suffered a contraction of $300 million of state-issued funding in the last year alone. The university system, which saw its budget steadily diminished for the majority of a decade, absorbed an equal reduction. In addition, the universities were refused the ability to raise tuition in order to compensate for the losses. Effectively, the public schools and universities have been left with no alternative but to shrink. They were compelled to fire employees and excise programs, or admit a deluge of new students without any corresponding increase in faculty and facilities. Under these policies, the universities shrank in absolute terms, or in proportion to operating capabilities, reducing departments and personnel, or admitting an overwhelming quantity of students.

State policies, however, have not been restricted to reducing funds. At the same time as the universities and schools are forced to contend with diminished budgets, the state is also redirecting both resources and students away from certain kinds of education, those degrees in arts, humanities, and social sciences, and toward programs in science and technology. In the midst of stripping $300 million from the existing universities, the state created an entirely new university, one "with an emphasis on science, technology, engineering and math" (Turner 2011). Originally, this new university, whose $30 million budget somehow appeared during a time of supposed fiscal crisis, was to be located on a campus that would be expropriated from the University of South Florida. When the administration of USF publicly opposed the plan, the institution was threatened with "a 58 percent reduction in its budget."[9]

With the beginning of 2013, Scott's administration announced plans to increase education spending in public schools and universities, restoring much of the funding previously lost. However, over half of that restoration would be contingent on meeting incentives such as the quantity of graduates produced and the "average wage of employed graduates" (Flechas 2013). Since, the rationale is that students in STEM fields earn more, this financial "relief" is clearly another means for pressuring universities to direct more students toward those fields. Concurrently, new funding is explicitly directed toward STEM facilities (ibid.).

As the creation of an entirely new STEM-oriented university and other STEM-related spending suggests, concomitant to the stresses placed on other components of the educational apparatus, state policy is meant to reallocate resources toward certain kinds of education. The emphasis toward STEM betrays the thin façade of a pragmatic response to the exigencies of the economy, revealing the fundamentally ideological character of these policies. The state is effectively using its power to impose an ideological curriculum, obstructing pathways to certain disciplines (arts, humanities, and social sciences) while facilitating traffic to others (STEM). State policy began to reflect the "desire to redirect state funds at public colleges from social science programs—like anthropology, psychology and political science—to physical sciences like technology, engineering and math" (Ruiz 2011). The policy merely reflects Governor Scott's view that education is exclusively for the purpose of securing employment, or, as he put it:

You know, we don't need a lot more anthropologists in the state. It's a great degree if people want to get it, but we don't need them here. I want to spend our dollars giving people science, technology, engineering, math degrees. That's what our kids need to focus all their time and attention on. Those type of degrees. So when they get out of school, they can get a job. (Weinstein 2011)

As one state senator explained, "When the No. 1 degree granted is psychology and the No. 2 degree is political science, maybe before we ask $100 million more of taxpayers we should redeploy what we have" (Colavecchio 2010). That redeployment would clearly divert resources by "directing it from programs like philosophy and Slavic languages to science, math and technology to help boost the state's biotechnology and research profile" (ibid.). Financial pressures may also be applied directly to students in order to divert them toward technical fields. A state task force created by Governor Scott proposed a tiered tuition system in which humanities, arts, and social science courses will cost more than STEM courses. As the chair of the task force explained, liberal arts programs would not be eliminated, "But you really better want to do it, because you may have to pay more" (Travis 2012).

SALTING THE EARTH

The state has pursued a policy of deliberately underfunding and overburdening the universities and public schools. Concurrent to that reduction, the state has also directed resources and students toward science, technology, engineering, and mathematics programs and away from humanities and social sciences. Again, in Althusser's theory, the school is crucial to the Ideological State Apparatus and its role in reproducing the relations of production, which ultimately permits the perpetuation of capitalism and the domination of the ruling class. Reducing the schools, or even overburdening them, would serve to undermine this fundamental aim. Since his theory would anticipate the expansion in size and quality of the school as an instrument of state ideology, the apparent reduction in this crucial component of the Ideological State Apparatus might be construed as an indication that Althusser is simply wrong, that his theory is fundamentally flawed. I suggest this is not the case. There is an explanatory gap in Althusser's theory stemming from his decidedly structuralist approach. Structuralism can, and often does, yield fascinating explanations. In this case, the structuralist approach is unable to account for the dynamism of the capitalist state and its responses to fluid conditions. For this reason, I turn to the humanist Marxism of Herbert Marcuse as solution to this Althusserian gap.

Why would the state impose burdens upon its primary instrument of interpellation, thus compromising its efficacy? Karl Marx noted that, by itself, class antagonism was insufficient to provoke a revolution. All of history, in the Marxist view, has been defined by conflict between the classes, but revolution requires more than mere antagonistic relations. Each mode of production generates its own sets of contradictions, the terms for a dialectical movement into the next mode of production. As example, the medieval nobility financially pressured the burghers who, in turn, formed the guilds and other financial associations to protect their wealth. These institutions were the primitive groundwork for capitalism and the bourgeoisie. Effectively, the feudal lords created the conditions for the demise of feudalism. The end of capitalism, for Marx, would require something more, a violent catalyst in the form of an economic upheaval. As he notes:

> And how does the bourgeoisie get over these crises? On the other hand by enforced destruction of a mass of productive forces; on the other, by the conquest of new markets, and by the more thorough exploitation of the old ones. That is to say, by paving the way for more extensive and destructive crises, and by diminishing the means whereby crises are prevented. (Marx and Engels, 1985, p. 86)

The movement of expansions and contractions would leave more and more people in desperate poverty until, with nothing left to lose, they would act in mass solidarity to seize the means of production and bring class antagonisms to an end. Of fundamental importance to this Marxist eschatology is the notion that economic crisis engenders the conditions for revolution, essentially shocking the proletariat into action. But here, in the midst of global capitalism with its crushing poverty and alienation, there is no revolution. In part this is because, as Marcuse (1969, p. 16) explains, the middle class has been bought off. It now pursues the false needs supplied by capitalism. This is one result of the counterrevolution.

Although most of Marcuse's writings on the subject appear during the tumult of the late 1960s, counterrevolution first emerges as a matter of serious consideration at least three decades earlier. In an essay entitled "A Study on Authority," Marcuse traces the philosophic justification for counterrevolt to the writings of Edmund Burke, Louis Bonald, and Joseph de Maistre. Indeed, Marcuse explains that the theory of counterrevolution begins with these authors before revolution has truly run its course, emerging "simultaneously with the French Revolution" (1972a, p. 111). As the revolution is underway, the theory of its reversal is being established. As revolutionary theory, with its liberal and egalitarian roots, was predicated on the autonomy of human beings, counterrevolutionary theory sought to undermine the source of that autonomy—reason. Accordingly, Marcuse explains that the theory of counterrevolution reinforces dependency by "engaging in a total defamation of human reason" (1972a, p. 114). That is, these early counterrevolutionary theorists sought to thwart the ascension of bourgeois values by gesturing to the insufficiency of individual reason in governing human affairs. Without this vital foundation, the rationale for a limited government was imperiled. The authority of kings, which represented the aggregated wisdom of history, was vastly superior and therefore more desirable than individual reason.

Marcuse returned to the issue of counterrevolution in considering why there had been no genuinely successful revolution. Capitalism seemed firmly entrenched in the West, despite some discontent among the young. The Soviet Union had effectively failed to exceed the parameters of capitalism. Instead, Marcuse found that the "revolution had turned against itself" (Bronner 1994, p. 236). Mired in some endless phase of supposed transition, the Russian brand of socialism bore all the signs of an increasingly strong "totalitarian administration" that "perpetuates the repressive economic and political features of the Soviet system" (Marcuse 1961, pp. 154–155). While he retained some dwindling hope for developments in Cuba and China, there had been no great unity among the proletariat, no uprising or programmatic disruption following the protests in the West. The "Great Refusal" had come to nothing. Despite the forces arrayed against it, capitalism managed to persevere, thrive, and permeate even greater material and ideological depths. Why? The answer, for Marcuse, is that capitalism reorganizes itself to repel its adversaries. This reorganization constitutes a set of deliberate strategies within the Establishment of capitalism designed to thwart avenues of dissent, nonconformity, and subversion—strategies of counterrevolution. The purpose of these manifold counterrevolutionary efforts are to stabilize the system by eliminating threats in advance, threats such as criticism and the development of revolutionary consciousness. As Marcuse (1969, p. 15) observes, "The power of corporate capitalism has stifled the emergence of such a consciousness and imagination; its mass media have adjusted the rational and emotional faculties to its market and its policies and steered them to defense of its domination." The ultimate goal is to convert and maintain the working class, which is the revolutionary class in Marxist thought, to a subordinate instrument. Through violence and seduction, the Establishment shapes the working class into an ideological ally until, finally, "by virtue of its sharing the stabilizing needs of the system, it has become a conservative, even counterrevolutionary force" (ibid., p. 16).

Of course, the *theory* of counterrevolution arises because of a discernible revolt in late eighteenth century France. Though they appear concomitant with that turmoil, the writings of Burke, Bonald, and de Maistre are reactionary, appearing in response to the turmoil and upheaval that brought the ancien regimé to a close. In the present, deploying the term 'counterrevolution' seems somewhat questionable, especially given that Marcuse acknowledges the dissolution of the Great Refusal. Nevertheless, he assures us that it is entirely appropriate, writing:

The "counterrevolution" is largely preventative and, in the Western world, altogether preventative. Here, there is no recent revolution to be undone, and there is none in the offing. And yet, fear of revolution which creates the common interest links the various stages and forms of the counterrevolution. It runs the whole gamut from parliamentary democracy via the police to state to open dictatorship. Capitalism reorganizes itself to meet the threat of a revolution which would the most radical of all historical revolutions. (Marcuse 1972b, pp. 1–2)

In the present, counterrevolution is preemptive, arising before revolution can be formulated. Capitalism anticipates possible threats, neutralizing them in advance. In that sense, we inhabit a state of permanent preemptive counterrevolution.

There are a variety of tactics at the disposal of the Establishment used to perpetuate counterrevolution. "Violence," Marcuse (1972b, p. 53) claims, "is the weapon of the Establishment; it operates everywhere, in the institutions and organization, in work and fun, on the streets and highways, and in the air." Beyond the physical violence of "massacres" and "torture" are the various ideological forces designed to draw the masses into the trappings of the consumer society by generating false needs for "constantly renewing the gadgets, devices, instruments, engines, offered to and imposed upon the people, for using these wares even at the danger of one's own destruction" (Marcuse 1969, p. 11). For Marcuse (ibid., p. 83), capitalism actively works toward the "moronization of children and adults alike" exactly because a population less able to reason is a population less able to resist, or imagine alternative possibilities to the prevailing order. In this regard, counterrevolution succeeds on the *subversion* of reason both in the sense of defaming its value, and actively stunting its development. Reason, Marcuse (1964, p. 123) explains, "is the subversive power," the means to challenge the pretext of ideology, and that is precisely why reason itself becomes the object of subversion. Thinking and behavior in late capitalism have become expressions of the false consciousness insinuated by the system and, in turn, contribute to the reproduction of the system (Marcuse 1964, p. 145).

For that reason, there is ultimately no divide or distance between the theory of counterrevolution and its practice. The practice of counterrevolution functions through the subversion of reason, while the theory proceeds through the defamation of reason. Yet that defamation is a practice that actively serves the political objective of preventing revolt. It is therefore clear that the defamation of reason is integral to the *practice* of counterrevolution. Defaming reason is essential to its subversion. In that sense, there is no distance between the defamation of reason and counterrevolutionary practice. The defamation of reason *is* counterrevolutionary practice. Hence, counterrevolution preemptively functions through restricting the acquisition, projecting a defamatory representation, and subverting the use made of reason.

In considering Marcuse's views on counterrevolution, why should the state shrink and overburden the schools and universities? Why direct resources away from subjects such as the arts, humanities, and social sciences? In Marcuse's view, "Art can indeed become a weapon in the class struggle by promoting changes in the prevailing consciousness" (Marcuse 1972b, p. 125). Or, as Althusser concurs, it is one of the "crucial tasks" in revolutionary theory "to conquer for science the majority of the Human Sciences, above all, the Social Sciences" and set about "linking them to the requirements and inventions of the practice of revolutionary class struggle" (Althusser 2001a, p. 5). The arts, humanities, and social sciences—all of which expressed an originally "bourgeois philosophy" of liberal education—harbor the potential for developing critical thinking and reason, or, as Marcuse (1972b, p. 28) demands, "assuming the vast task of *political education*, dispelling the false and mutilated consciousness of the people so that they themselves experience their condition, and its abolition, as vital need, and apprehend the ways and means of their liberation."

Why, then, direct resources toward the natural sciences, technology, engineering, and math? Because, as Governor Scott of Florida wrote, the universities and their graduates must become clients of industry, and "increase their STEM research productivity that can be commercialized and expanded into new economic opportunities, and build strong relationships with the business community to expand services such as business incubators" (Solochek 2011). Scott continued by stating that, as universities become appendages of industry and students receive technical training, "companies will recognize our state as the best place to tap into the talent that will allow business to grow and succeed" (Scott 2011). As Marcuse and Althusser both attest, the intellectual fertility of the arts and humanities represent a potential threat, especially during an economic crisis, whereas the disciplines desired by the state—natural sciences, technology, engineering, and mathematics—are more easily commodifiable, and render individuals more exploitable. Generally, the disciplines of STEM are not disposed toward the criticism of the state or the prevailing relations of production. While scientists and engineers have undoubtedly been known to make important contributions, science and engineering do not make social or political relations the object of critique. Albert Einstein, for example, earned a reputation as a socially conscientious scientist. Indeed, many scientists are concerned with the uses of technology and the environmental crises that plague modern society. In many cases, these are also scientists who had the advantage of exposure to political education. Furthermore, the explicit objective of Scott's (and others') emphasis on STEM is to serve corporate rather than social interests. In that regard, I feel it is quite safe to say that Rick Scott's education agenda has nothing to do with creating environmentalists or Einsteins. Rather, precisely because they are more commodifiable vocations, they are more easily put into the service of reproducing the relations of production.

The deprivation of resources in the arts and human sciences, and the diversion of those resources toward technical fields, ought to be understood as a counterrevolutionary means for aborting the critical intellect, aborting the faculties for social and political criticism. STEM fields have no bearing on the inspiration of social or political consciousness. Training more individuals in these fields, and fewer in those that emphasize critical thinking, is likely to result in a greater number of pliable technicians and fewer dissenters. Marcuse (1969, p. 57) explains that, through political education, a consciousness can be developed in the minds of the exploited to "loosen the hold of enslaving needs over their existence." This is precisely what is prevented by the emphasis on nomothetic disciplines such as those pertaining to STEM, and the exclusion of potentially normative fields in the arts, humanities, and social sciences. In fact, Marcuse states that without political education, the very notion of liberation becomes the "mass basis of counterrevolution" (ibid.). For these reasons, the state's policy of shrinking and overburdening the public schools and universities, representing the gap within Althusser's theory, can be accounted for in terms of counterrevolution. Marcuse (1972b, pp. 27–28) avers that whereas education held the promise of creating a more rational society, it has increasingly been subverted toward producing technicians that serve, not the promise of progress, but the profit of "the established society." Indeed, the claims that retooling education toward STEM fields will create a greater quantity of good jobs seems particularly dubious. It appears more likely to result in a devaluation of the individual worker in those fields, rendering those workers less individually crucial and, therefore, cheaper to employ. As Marx alerts us:

> The worker becomes all the poorer the more wealth he produces, the more his production increases in power and range. The worker becomes an ever-cheaper commodity the more commodities he creates. With the increasing *value* of the world of things proceeds in direct proportion the *devaluation* of the world of men. (Marx 1988, p. 71).

While the rationale behind this curricular restructuring is to produce workers in technically sophisticated fields, the ultimate goal seems to be the increase in the number of workers in these fields, which would likely have the result of devaluing trained individuals in those fields, leading to lower wages. The larger effect, beyond mere employment in STEM industries, is to reorganize the educational apparatuses, effectively stunting the critical capabilities of the educated. In this manner, the criticism of the relations of production, the iniquities of which are acutely transparent during an economic crisis, is subverted before it can even form.

The curriculum has been reshaped, under the guise of economic necessity, in order to produce more technicians to serve the aims of the system, and, by eliminating the faculties of dissent before they can even develop, fewer critics. And that is precisely how this state policy toward the institutions of education has to be understood, as a strategy of counterrevolution that aims at aborting the intellect. As Lenin (1987, p. 69) noted, "Without a revolutionary theory, there can be no revolutionary movement." The state strategy is meant to eliminate that revolutionary theory, never mind practice, before it can develop. Economic crises lend themselves to revolutionary possibilities. The policy response strikes preemptively, salting the soil of dissent. Shrinking and overburdening the schools does nothing to defuse the efficacy of interpellation, and in a crisis it is of paramount importance to neutralize the conditions that engender revolutionary consciousness, dulling the critical faculties of the intellect. In effect, the various efforts to deprive schools and universities of funding, or burden them with too many students, are means for eliminating the embryo of social and political criticism from being conceived, a counterrevolutionary preemption against the possibility of dissent. As the state saddles the school with the demands of supernumerary students and deprives it of resources, students themselves are funneled away from the humanities, arts, and social sciences—disciplines that historically pertain to critical thinking and, potentially, dissent, and toward science, technology, engineering, and math—disciplines that are not directly germane to social criticism and are far more easily commodified and exploited. Represented through the perspective of Herbert Marcuse's views, the present strategies of the state ought not to be understood as attacks on the school as much as attacks on philosophy, counterrevolutionary tactics that shift students away from developing the faculties of criticism and toward disciplines subservient to the relations of production and the ruling class.

PRELUDE TO FASCISM

Although this chapter has emphasized the manipulation of resources to promote a specific, technical curriculum in the state of Florida, these counterrevolutionary tactics are by no means exclusive to the administration of Rick Scott, or the territory he governs. Wisconsin Governor Scott Walker, another pro-business Republican, reduced education spending in his state by nearly $900 million (P. Anderson 2012). Walker simultaneously proposed a plan to make university funding conditional upon "how well those institutions prepare students to take available and needed jobs in Wisconsin" (Hall and Derby 2012). In essence, artificially scarce funding will become contingent upon the acquiescence of universities to the demands of Wisconsin employers.[10] In North Carolina, Governor Pat McCrory announced a plan to reallocate university funding based on the demonstration of graduate employment. Therefore, universities that promoted employable disciplines, presumably within the STEM fields, would receive the most funding (Rosenberg 2013). As McCrory, echoing Rick Scott's sentiments, explained, "If you want to take gender studies, that's fine, go to a private school. But I don't want to subsidize that if it's not going to get someone a job" (Bruni 2013).

Of course, the diversion of resources toward technical fields is certainly not peculiar to Republican politicians and administrations. The administration of Democratic Governor Deval Patrick of Massachusetts has declared the objective of ensuring "that all students are educated in STEM fields, which will enable them to pursue post-secondary degrees or careers in these areas" (Mass.gov 2012). Indeed, the Massachusetts plan goes beyond merely introducing students to these fields, and includes an explicit ideological component in which awareness of the benefits of STEM are first raised. As the state report makes clear, once students are made aware of STEM, "individual interests can be sparked" (STEM Advisory Council 2012, p. 11).[11] Meanwhile, in Texas, the Republican Party's official platform document of 2012 explicitly called for eliminating critical thinking skills in state schools, candidly stating:

> We oppose the teaching of Higher Order Thinking Skills (HOTS) (values clarification), critical thinking skills and similar programs that are simply a relabeling of Outcome-Based Education (OBE) (mastery learning) which focus on behavior modification and have the purpose of challenging the student's fixed beliefs and undermining parental authority. (Republican Party of Texas 2012, p. 12)

Economic crisis precipitated these policies. However, economic crisis did not necessitate a reduction in education funds and diversion of resources to technical fields. Instead, such crises represent a greater possibility of criticism against capitalism and that is why counterrevolutionary strategies have been directed toward the manipulation of curriculum. The economic crisis was merely a pretext for ideological reorganization and subduing the potential for dissent.

There is good reason to be concerned with these policies, even if one is not a Marxist or an opponent of capitalism. In Marcuse's view, the range of tactics employed in the counterrevolution—torture, massacres, and, above all, the subversion of reason—signal a possible shift away from liberal-capitalism, and potentially signal a turn toward the even more pernicious appearance of fascism. As Marcuse (1972b, p. 24) states, "Decisive is rather whether the present phase of the (preventative) counterrevolution (its democratic-constitutional phase) does not prepare the soil for a subsequent fascist phase." Hence, the abortion of the intellect may constitute a counterrevolutionary prelude to fascism. In that regard, the strategy rests on the invocation of patriotic ideals designed to replace individual, and therefore liberal, concerns with fascination for the state and its concerns (Marcuse 1972a, pp. 116-117). In their denunciation of liberalism, Mussolini and Gentile (2011, p. 297) write, "Against individualism, the Fascist conception is for the State; and it is for the individual in so far as he coincides with the State, which is the conscience and universal will of man in his historical existence." Meanwhile, the justifications for shifting curriculum have invoked the good of the state as hanging in the balance, if not the foremost concern. In crafting the state's policy, Rick Scott explained, "It is vital for the future of Florida's economy that we meet the need for a STEM-educated work force. Failing to meet this challenge will be costly to our state for decades" (Turner 2012). In effect, the value of education, in this view, lies not in its ability to improve the individual as a human being, or the quality of civilization, but in maximizing the productivity of each individual toward contributing to the good of the state. Accordingly, the arts, humanities, and social sciences are counterproductive, while science, technology, engineering, and mathematics benefit the priorities of the state. State Senator Don Gaetz claimed that the failure to produce "the right graduates" is what has made "Florida a 'second tier' state in attracting companies" (Z. Anderson 2011). The interests of the state have become the priority, and education, according to these policies, ought to serve those interests.

Political education has become shrouded at the midnight of dissent. There may yet be a dawn, but such a respite is never guaranteed. Ultimately, the trajectory of the counterrevolution remains to be seen. Though it may never reach that point, identifying its manifestations and examining its effects are imperative precisely because of its potential to conclude with fascism. Praxis has always been and remains an extraordinarily difficult issue for Marxist thinkers. Ever since the scribbling of the Eleventh Thesis that became perhaps Marx's most solemn admonishment, Marxists have struggled to measure the imperative for action against the potential for merely furthering the exploitative, alienating, and destructive power of capitalism. If Althusser is correct, then such theorists are only in the process of becoming revolutionary; they always bear the anchor of the bourgeoisie, the heavy trace of capitalism. Nevertheless, Lenin's call for political education remains essential, and, therefore, the representation of policy decisions, budget reductions and resource reallocations, ought to be situated in terms of class struggle. These are more than fiscal decisions; state power is being exerted in order to shape the curriculum. As I turn next to examine the representation of intellectuals, it becomes apparent how the defamatory representation of reason actively serves its subversion.

NOTES

1. Of course, as I will demonstrate in greater detail below, Florida is hardly alone in its assault on education. Governor Scott Walker of Wisconsin has unveiled a similar plan. Republican presidential candidate Ron Paul consistently called for eliminating the entire Department of Education (Bingham 2011). There are plentiful examples to draw on, and by no means are they all restricted to Republican-controlled governments or Republican politicians.

2. Education was not the only area affected by Scott's budget. In unveiling his budget, Scott explained, "Reviewing a governmental budget is much like going through the attic in an old home. You come across some priceless things you need to protect. But there are a lot of odd things someone once thought we needed. Much of it we've outgrown. And it just doesn't fit anymore. Over the last month, I've spent a lot of time in that attic. And I'm cleaning it out" (Caputo and Bousquet 2011). Apparently, that also included cleaning out 8,700 employees from the State of Florida "attic" (Padgett 2011).

3. One study estimated that tax revenues in Florida were decreased by approximately "$5.6 billion or 14% of its 2005 tax revenues" (Lutz, Molloy, and Shan 2010, 3).

4. Althusser himself rejected humanist forms of Marxism, the kind that Marcuse could be said to represent. Despite this probable objection, Althusser's own structuralist approach is blind in this area and requires a supplement.

5. These factors include the strain of wars in Afghanistan, Iraq, and the more globally diffuse "war on terrorism;" massive bankruptcies of fraudulent corporations such as Enron, Worldcom, and Tyco; market deregulation and tax decreases; and unrestricted oil speculation.

6. Schiller (2010) reports that, adjusting for inflation, the price of existing homes increased by nearly 200 percent between the year 2000 and 2005. This bubble largely corrected itself with a corresponding 200 percent decrease between 2007 and 2009.

7. Economists and pundits have argued about whether or not to call this contraction a recession or the more serious term, depression. In any event, Marx spoke in general terms of the cyclical tendency in capitalism toward expansion and contraction.

8. During the 2010–2012 term, Republicans outnumbered Democrats in both houses of the state legislature by a margin of two to one.

9. DiSalvo (2012) reports the plan was conceived by the outgoing president of the state senate who represents the district in which the campus is based.

10. As indicated earlier, Florida is beginning to follow this model.

11. The state of Massachusetts does not appear to have a similar plan for raising awareness and sparking interests in the humanities or arts.

Chapter Three

Inhuman Minds

Structural Representations of Intellectuals under the Counterrevolution

LABORS OF THOUGHT

An intellectual is generally thought of as a person whose labor is related in some way to the life of the mind. That might beg the question as to whether or not a construction worker, in addition to more traditionally associated vocations such as academics, could also be an intellectual. Can a prostitute also be an intellectual? Clearly, some imagination or creativity is useful in those professions. Max Weber (1946, p. 176) defines intellectuals as those who "by virtue of their peculiarity have special access to certain achievements considered to be 'culture values.'" Of course, it remains unclear as to what constitutes that peculiarity, or those achievements. There is no governing body, formal or otherwise, that administers credentials to intellectuals, no certification, badge, or even diploma that deems an individual accordingly. Designations such as those indicated by an academic degree do not necessarily confer the status of being an intellectual. Moreover, to the best of my knowledge, no academic institution has posted any advertisement soliciting employment for an intellectual even though such a person would seem to be useful. At a certain level, it seems less than clear as to when a person is laboring with his or mind. I am, after all, contemplating these ideas, but I am also physically typing them. Am I an intellectual, dealing in ideas, or am I a typist? Tibor Huszar (1976, p. 79) points out that the meaning of the term varies widely according to different cultures, and, even within the same culture, may contain numerous variants such as "mental workers, cultured strata, intellectuals, people with a free profession, and so on." To be com-

31

pletely forthright, I am not exactly sure what constitutes an intellectual in any precise terms. Nevertheless, we can understand quite clearly what an intellectual means for those such as Raymond Aron, Mark Lilla, and Thomas Sowell. In their view, intellectuals, a categorical term saddled with a distinctly pejorative character, are those with whom they disagree upon matters germane to society and politics. For these writers, and others, 'intellectuals' are identical with politically vocal leftists. Under this view, intellectuals are those who might have the audacity to suggest society might be improvable, and politics can be arranged according to less exploitative principles.

Assaults on intellectuals, both rhetorical and physical, existed long before capitalism. Perhaps the most recognizable case is that of Socrates. Before his trial and execution for corrupting the youth and denying the gods of Athens, the founder of Western philosophy had already been depicted as a teacher of both absurdities and sinister skills in Aristophanes' *Clouds*. Ominously, in the final scene, Socrates' school, the *phrontisterion*, is burned to the ground and he is chased from view. Hence, this great intellectual figure is persecuted in both fiction and reality. Yet, even before the fate of Socrates, the more enigmatic figure of Pythagoras had already suffered his demise at the hands of an intolerant mob. The Pythagoreans were a secretive society, not so secret that their existence was unknown, but selective in their admissions. Rites and mysteries were privileges of the initiated, and this reserved knowledge and exclusivity combined to create jealousy and fear among the unfamiliar. At the Greek colony of Croton, a mob, fearful that the secretive Pythagoreans harbored tyrannical ambitions, was incited to violence by a young aristocrat named Cylon who had been refused admission into the society (Diogenes Laertius 1901, p. 354). They burned down the home of a Pythagorean named Milo, and killed Pythagoras himself.

In the present, intellectuals as a broad category, remain the object of derision. More specifically, academics appear to be the target of particularly pronounced ridicule. Beyond the confines of academia, the labeling of someone as a "professor" seems almost universally contemptuous. During their contest for United States Senate, Scott Brown (R-MA), the Tea Party–backed incumbent, repeatedly referred to his opponent, Elizabeth Warren, as "Professor Warren" as a means to "paint her as an out-of-touch Cambridge elitist" (Vennochi 2012). Outside the halls of power, we are also told that professors are nearly uniform in their leftism, and harbor designs on insidiously converting impressionable students away from the orthodoxy of their parents. Kors and Silverglate (1998, p. 4), for example, argue that "self-appointed progressives," inspired by Herbert Marcuse, have covertly established "a tyranny that is far more dangerous than the relatively innocuous parietal rules of ages past" at universities across the country. Sohrab Ahmari (2012) contends that the university is "the most authoritarian institution in America," and clearly identifies that condition with the ascent of progressive values, suggesting that "conservatives and libertarians are especially vulnerable" in this environment. And, more famously, it has been the staid tradition of College Republicans on different campuses to establish lists of "liberal professors" in an attempt to "speak out for students who may have been victims of the bias" (Green 2009). The intellectual, and the professor in particular, are, under this view, somehow markedly different than the rest of the decent folk out there.

Within contemporary conservative political discourse the term "intellectual" has assumed a pejorative tenor and only seems presentable through an accompanying, if implicit, sneer. Political figures, and even some academics, have expressed a hostile attitude toward the figure of the intellectual. Of course, this derision is not universally applicable to conservatives, many of whom are themselves intellectuals and fully appreciate the use of reason. Likewise, anti-intellectualism, by which I mean the derogatory representation of an intellectual, has sometimes been a symptom of radicals and leftists. Indeed, elements within the New Left exhibited the "anti-intellectualism" of more conservative capitalist elements (1972b, p. 129). During one exchange with members of the Students for a Democratic Society, detailed in *Playboy*, Marcuse cautioned against dispensing with the fundamentals of education, "the basics of history, economics, psychology, philosophy, and so on" (Horowitz 1970) When the students retorted that the "white man's economic courses" were irrelevant for a black man in a revolutionary situation, Marcuse admonished, "I detect here what I have found on many campuses I have visited: a growing anti-intellectual attitude among the students. There is no contradiction between intelligence and revolution. Why are you afraid of being intelligent?" (ibid.).

While the work of analyzing the anti-intellectualism of the left is also important, the aim here is to assess the structure of anti-intellectualism as a symptom of the counterrevolution. Because the left is more generally associable with systemic criticism and dissent, I focus exclusively on disparaging conservative representations of intellectuals. Regardless if the term employed is actually "intellectual," or any of its equally denigrating derivatives such as "academic," "professorial," or "intelligentsia," the term is meant to evoke and disparage the holder of a dissenting and probably leftist view. The strategy has been quite successful. As one of my colleagues professed, there is probably something wrong with anyone who would assume for oneself the title of intellectual. To do so would seem conceited, but then conceit appears to be consistent with the profile of the intellectual according to the conservative commentators.

How is the intellectual represented under the conditions of the counterrevolution? How does that representation serve counterrevolutionary aims? What end is served by the defamation of intellectuals, and what is the structure of that defamation? As Herbert Marcuse reminds us, counterrevolutionary theory and, therefore, practice acts on "the total defamation of reason." As there is no distance between the theory of counterrevolution and its practice—since both function according to the subversion of reason—the treatment of intellectuals is an important consideration in evaluating the politics of reason (or the present state of counterrevolution). Hence, the faculties of reason are made to atrophy by undermining the faculties of the intellect before they can even develop. Furthermore, as I will demonstrate here, this defamation is also supported through the disparaging depictions of those aligned with reason in its most critical form, the purveyors of criticism. The discourse of conservative anti-intellectualism prevalent in late capitalism contributes to the production of counterrevolution by dehumanizing the intellectual.

But how does the representation of the "intellectual" serve the aims of undermining criticism and dissent? In conducting this analysis, I draw heavily on the semiotic method of Algirdas Julien Greimas. In particular, I employ what is known as the Greimassian or semiotic rectangle. Although Greimas remains largely unknown to American political science and philosophy, his work represents a useful form of narrative and discourse analysis. In the following section, I will offer an account of Greimassian semiology and production of the semiotic rectangle. As my approach to Greimassian semiotics is heavily influenced by Fredric Jameson's intervention, his explanations will also serve as a source of mediation. The third section details anti-intellectual rhetoric from conservative sources, including both academics and politicians. The academics include figures such as Leo Strauss, Raymond Aron, Paul Johnson, Mark Lilla, and Thomas Sowell. Despite their common misgivings about "intellectuals," these two groupings of conservative figures take vastly opposite approaches in their criticisms. As I will demonstrate, the conclusions reached by the academics form antipodal positions with those expressed by politicians in reference to the power exhibited by (leftist) intellectuals in present society. In the fourth section, I schematize the structure of anti-intellectualism using Greimas's semiotic square, demonstrating how the structural opposition between the positions taken by academics and politicians synthesize within the complex term of dehumanization. Hence, my argument is that the larger counterrevolutionary strategy of defaming reason relies in part on the dehumanization of the intellectual.

NOTES ON THE GREIMASSIAN RECTANGLE

The ideas of the structuralist semiotician Algirdas Julien Greimas remain sorely underrepresented, if not altogether absent, within the disciplines of political science and political philosophy. As such, the examples of his influence are quite limited. Ole Waever (1990, p. 336) deploys Greimassian semiology in his review of Walter Carlsnaes's book, *The Language of Foreign Policy*, asserting, "Meaning is internal to language and created through textual practice." Grunberg (1990, p. 450) cites one of Greimas' contributions to the field of semiotics in his development of the term "actants." Harris (1982, p. 37) invokes the utility of Greimassian thought as a means for interpreting the Constitution of the United States and constitutional issues, though this invocation remains essentially preliminary rather than applied. Aside from these examples, very little use of Greimas's work is made within political science or political philosophy. His thought remains largely confined to literary criticism, despite its potential value to the social sciences. This absence is not necessarily without cause; Greimas's work, steeped in the argot and modeling of semiotics might reasonably seem like an esoteric pseudoscience. It can also be just difficult to grasp without already having an extensive background in structuralism. Moreover, Greimas's greatest contribution, the so-called "semiotic square," might appear bankrupt of normative value.[1] So, while Greimas has been recognized within politically attentive fields, such as literary criticism, sociology, and legal theory, his work has been neglected within political science itself. The obscurity of Greimas's work within political science and political philosophy is really a lost opportunity as the value of his interpretive framework is ideally suited for the examination of rhetoric and discourse, essential facets of politics.

Indeed, it is Fredric Jameson, a literary theorist, who is probably most responsible for extolling the virtues of the Greimassian rectangle in political and social interpretation. As Wegner (2009, p. 215) writes, "Greimas's rectangle becomes an ideal means of illustrating the narrative operation Jameson names 'a symbolic act, whereby real social contradictions, insurmountable in their own terms, find a purely formal resolution in the aesthetic realm.'" Put differently, the semiotic rectangle highlights the terms of ideological closure and points, thereby, to a dialectical possibility for moving on. And far from being devoid of normative value, the rectangle provides the means for a structural schematization that permits judgment. Jameson notes:

> The semiotic rectangle becomes a vital instrument for exploring the semantic and ideological intricacies of the text—not so much because, as in Greimas' own work, it yields the objective possibilities according to which landscape and the physical elements, say, must necessarily be perceived, as rather because it maps the limits of a specific ideological consciousness and marks the conceptual points beyond which that consciousness cannot go, and between which it is condemned to oscillate. (Jameson 1981, p. 47)

In that sense, Jameson (1981, p. 83) explains that the "validity" of semiotics in general, and the Greimassian rectangle in particular, rests on its usefulness to "model ideological closure and to articulate the workings of binary oppositions." It is an effective cartographical instrument, mapping the horizons of ideological discourse and, in that regard, is decidedly relevant for normative theory.

Structure refers to relationships within a given system such as an ideology or a game. As Jameson (1981, p. 36) puts it, structure is "the entire system of *relationships*," and supplies the various possibilities, horizons for a given discourse. Greimas (1979, p. 31) describes the terms of a game accordingly, "One is free to enter, but not to exit. The player can neither quit the game— he would be a coward—nor cease to obey the rules—he would be a cheater." The term "game" serves quite aptly as a metaphor representing what Greimas calls "normative systems," including the specialized environment of political arenas. The structure of a normative system, whether a game or political discourse, establishes the parameters of what ought to be desirable from what ought to be objects of aversion. Greimas (1979, p. 34) explains that in these normative systems, "all that is not prescribed is forbidden, and vice versa." Formed by the relationship of opposing elements, structure is constitutive, defining "the fundamental mode of existence of an individual and society, and subsequently the conditions of existence of semiotic objects" (Greimas 1987, p. 48). Since structure is formed on the basis of opposition, it necessarily harbors normative demands; one term in the relationship is privileged, the other is neglected if not outright contemptible. Importantly, the value of a term, whether privileged or not, extends no further than discourse. That one term should be favored over another is only an expression of the game or other normative system, and not any transcendental truth.

Establishing these horizons, which is the role of the semiotic rectangle, exposes not merely the rules of the game, but an image of its aims and objectives as well. The rectangle commences from the establishment of a simple binary opposition, two elemental components or "minimal units of signification" designated "semes" (Schleifer 1987, p. 12). These are represented by the variables "s_1" and "s_2" (See Fig. 3-1). Initially, semes stand in a relationship of contrariness to one another (Greimas 1987, p. 49). The specificity of the term "contrary," and its subsequent distinction from other kinds of oppositional relations is crucial. Contrariness indicates a total opposition. Indeed, the two contraries, despite their exhaustive opposition are, nevertheless, bound together within the confines of a system. Jameson's (1987, p. xiv) explanation of the relationship between black and white is instructive. While totally opposed to one another, they remain bound by a relationship to the broader category of color.

Here, we might substitute the terminology of color for that of power, strong (s_1) and weak (s_2). These contrary semes, strong and weak, are both referents of power (See Fig. 3-2).

$$S_1 \longleftrightarrow S_2$$

Figure 3.1.

Transition from the Contrary to the Contradictory

Proceeding from the original binary, each seme harbors the terms of its own negation; they are always already present. Greimas (1987, p. 49) explains that the semes "point to the existence of their contradictory terms." Hence, the seme negates itself resulting in a new term, the *contradictory*. Whereas the semes within the contrary relation are antithetically opposed to one another, the contradictory relation is distinct insofar as it merely indicates otherness. This accommodates opposition, but gestures toward a much broader category. In comparison to the original contrary seme, the contradictory indicates the position of "not x," instead of exclusively "against x." This is what Jameson (1987, p. xiv) means when he writes, "the two supplementary slots of what logic calls a 'contradictory,' where $\sim s_1$ and $\sim s_2$ are the simple negatives of the two dominant terms, but include far more than either."

Expanding from the original relation of contrariness, wherein strong and weak opposed one another, the rectangle now includes the contradictory terms. Strong (s_1) is contradicted by that which is not strong ($\sim s_1$) while weak (s_2) is contradicted by all that includes not weak ($\sim s_2$). The two contradictory semes also form a relation of contrariness with one another as not strong is antipodal to not weak (See Fig. 3).

Finally, the two sets of contrary semes establish larger synthetic positions of "conceptual enlargements" (Jameson 1987, p. xiv). The privileged term in the system, that which is invested with signification is the "complex term" (S) (Greimas 1987, p. 51). The opposing, "neutral term" ($\sim$S) is "taken as an absolute absence of meaning" (Greimas 1987, p. 49). Hence, the semes of strong (s_1) and weak (s_2) indicate a complex term denoting forms or degrees of power (S). The contradictory semes of not weak ($\sim s_2$) and not strong ($\sim s_1$) gesture toward a neutral term of powerlessness or degrees of non-power ($\sim$S).

In order to proceed with mapping the structure of anti-intellectualism in conservative discourse it will be necessary to examine the elements of rhetoric used to represent intellectuals. As I will demonstrate in the next section, the denigration of intellectuals is quite closely associated with the signification of power just detailed.

$$(\text{strong})\ s_1 \longleftrightarrow s_2\ (\text{weak})$$

Figure 3.2.

MONSTERS WALK AMONG US...

I suggest here that there are two distinctive depictions of intellectuals within conservative discourse, depictions that inadvertently or otherwise serve the ends of counterrevolution. The first category consists of commentary about intellectuals authored by those who might very well be classified as intellectuals themselves: conservative academics and writers. The second category contains observations on intellectuals made by American politicians. Both of these depictions refer to the level of potency, or lack thereof, that intellectuals possess. In the various warnings about intellectuals originating with academic figures such as Leo Strauss, Raymond Aron, Paul Johnson, Mark Lilla, and Thomas Sowell, intellectuals are depicted as excessively potent. Conversely, commentary from politicians is as likely to disparage intellectuals as constituting a dangerous fifth column, but only under the terms of being woefully impotent and pathetically ineffectual.

Surplus of Power (s_1)

Perhaps the most curious aspect of conservative anti-intellectual discourse is that much of it emanates from academics. It seems that some of the harshest criticism of intellectuals begins with those who might easily be characterized within that same category. Of course, a number of these writers tend to repudiate that label, which, in their writings, seems almost exclusively applicable to leftists. Many contemporary academic admonishments against (left) intellectuals take some of their bearings from the writings of Leo Strauss, who was once called "the greatest writer of epic political theory" in the twentieth century (Gunnell 1985, p. 339). Although Strauss would certainly not have considered himself anti-intellectual in the most general sense, his writings betray a disdain for the socially caustic potential of heterodox thinking and the individuals who promote such views.[2] Controversially, he concluded that the vulgar masses would be intolerant of the philosophers' truth. Authors of philosophic texts were, therefore, compelled to conceal the highest truths "exclusively between the lines" (Strauss 1952, p. 25).[3] In this manner of esoteric writing, a philosopher could communicate her views to the trustworthy while taking the necessary precautions to avoid persecution. While the vulgar many represent a danger to the philosopher, Strauss also

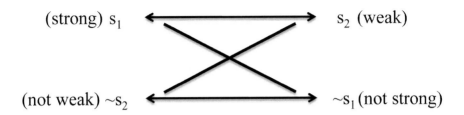

(strong) s_1 s_2 (weak)

(not weak) $\sim s_2$ $\sim s_1$ (not strong)

Figure 3.3.

finds the inverse to be true. The philosopher also poses a grave, destructive threat to the society he or she inhabits. As Strauss notes:

> Philosophy or science, the highest activity of man, is the attempt to replace opinion about "all things" by knowledge of "all things"; but opinion is the element of society; philosophy or science is therefore the attempt to dissolve the element in which society breathes, and thus it endangers society. (Strauss 1959, p. 221)

While the activities of the mind represent the apex of human life, they are also thoroughly dangerous. Society is threatened by the subversive displacement of its views. Accordingly, the philosopher, or at least the decent philosopher, should have no place expressing truth in public discourse precisely because "there are basic truths which would not be pronounced in public by any decent man, because they would do harm to many people" (Strauss 1954, p. 36).

Writing in the 1950s, Raymond Aron found that his contemporaries had been intoxicated by the opiate of Marxism. While they may initially harbor good intentions, their narcissism leads intellectuals "to connive ultimately at terror and autocracy" (Aron 1957, p. 212). As with Strauss, Aron expresses the view that intellectuals possess a surfeit of power. He writes, "to all this the intellectuals as a whole react more passionately than the other social categories, because they have higher ambitions and more extensive means of action" (ibid., p. 218). In this view, therefore, intellectuals are more capable of promoting their agenda than other groups, and, for Aron, this clearly meant the promotion of communism. Thus, he explains, the intellectual "mobilizes the masses, trains them for battle, takes them to schools, urges them on to work, teaches them the 'truth'" (Aron p. 303). Whereas Strauss was concerned with the idea that some intellectual figures might actually possess dangerous truths, Aron seems confident that communist intellectuals were imposters of truth.

Paul Johnson appears to completely discount the plausibility that intellectuals have any relationship to the truth. Indeed, he claims that any randomly

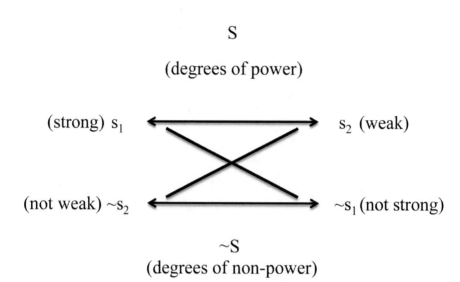

S

(degrees of power)

(strong) s_1 s_2 (weak)

(not weak) $\sim s_2$ $\sim s_1$ (not strong)

$\sim$S
(degrees of non-power)

Figure 3.4.

selected group of people would have equally valid ideas when compared with those belonging to the intelligentsia. It would seem that, for Johnson, the title of "intellectual" is purely nominal, perhaps the emptiest of signifiers. However, in his assessment of figures such as Jean-Jacques Rousseau, Mary Shelley, Karl Marx, Bertolt Brecht, Jean-Paul Sartre, Bertrand Russell, Noam Chomsky, and others, Johnson echoes the sentiment that critics of orthodoxy are extremely dangerous. He writes, "There seems to be, in the life of many millenarian intellectuals, a sinister climacteric, a cerebral menopause, which might be termed the Flight of Reason" (Johnson 1988, p. 341). In this view, intellectuals are clever people whose reasoning comes to an abrupt end. Of course, the problem is not merely that intellectuals have ceased menstruating reason (if I follow Johnson correctly).[4] Rather, these thinkers have been responsible for the enormity of human suffering since at least the Enlightenment. As Johnson explains:

> One of the principal lessons of our tragic century, which has seen so many millions of innocent lives sacrificed in schemes to improve the lot of humanity, is—beware intellectuals. Not merely should they be kept well away from the levers of power, they should also be objects of particular suspicion when they seek to offer collective advice. Beware committees, conferences and leagues of intellectuals. Distrust public statements issued from their serried ranks. Discount their verdicts on political leaders and important events. (Johnson 1988, p. 342)

Moreover, Johnson (ibid.) explains that because they tend to be like-minded, intellectuals are "dangerous" and generate "destructive courses of action." Although he does not explicitly concur with the view that they bear anything like truth, Mark Lilla does agree that intellectuals are a dangerous lot. Despite vast political differences between them, Lilla equates left intellectuals, such as Benjamin, Foucault, and Derrida with actual members of the Nazi Party, Martin Heidegger and Carl Schmitt. As Stoekl (2004, 90) notes in his review of Lilla's text, the reader is misled to "conclude that these disparate authorities are, in the end, remarkably similar in their temptations and intellectual misdeeds." In this manner, Nazi intellectuals are shaped into instruments for the purpose of condemning leftists who purportedly suffer the same malady of "philotyranny," the love of despotic regimes. Although no evidence is furnished to demonstrate Benjamin, Foucault, or Derrida supported an actual tyranny (thus leaving only the aforementioned right-wing intellectuals, Schmitt and Heidegger, susceptible to that folly), Lilla writes:

> Distinguished professors, gifted poets, and influential journalists summoned their talents to convince all who would listen that modern tyrants were liberators and that their unconscionable crimes were noble, when seen in the proper perspective. (Lilla 2001, p. 198)

Despite this dearth of support for the claim that Benjamin, Foucault, or Derrida spoke on behalf of tyranny, Lilla concludes that the ideas of intellectuals "had to be protected from the world, but they also must be kept from worldly political affairs, which are properly the concern of others—of citizens, statesmen, of men of action" (Lilla 2001, p. 43).[5]

Thomas Sowell readily agrees with this characterization of intellectuals as dangerous. Usefully, he first draws a distinction between the intellectual and more practical vocations. Hence, engineers, physicians, and computer scientists cannot be intellectuals, who exclusively labor in ideas. Sowell insists that the various problems caused by intellectuals (and there are many) are due to the fact they meddle in affairs for which they have no business. As he puts it, "the point is that many *did not stay within their respective fields*" (Sowell 2001, p. 12).[6] Thus, Noam Chomsky, despite the fact that he has exhausted decades studying social and political problems, is a nuisance and a danger because he dared to comment "beyond the realm of linguistics," his certified area of expertise (Sowell 2009, p. 284). Likewise, Bertrand Russell, surely one of the greatest philosophers of the twentieth century, made "inflammatory comments on things for which he had no qualification" (Sowell 2009, p. 287).

The problem, however, is not merely that intellectuals wander from the confines of their clearly demarcated disciplines.[7] As with Lilla, for Sowell, intellectuals represent a "great social danger" because their ideas do not require external validation. Intellectuals are "ultimately unaccountable to the external world," he continues (Sowell 2009, p. 8). This suggests an inordinate amount of latitude and power to exercise. Indeed, Sowell (2009, p. 96) states that the "vision of the left is one of surrogate decision-making."[8] In other words, intellectuals are unaccountable and "totalitarian" (ibid., p. 96). In fact, intellectuals apparently imagine themselves entitled "to judge, pontificate to, or direct a whole society" (ibid., p. 155). Furthermore, threats persist in the mundane world of the academy and the school. Intellectuals can promote "their opinions in the classroom to a captive audience of students, operating in a smaller arena but in a setting with little chance of serious challenge" (ibid., p. 288). In the final analysis, the hazards of intellectuals are potentially cataclysmic. As Sowell avers:

> As we have already seen, especially in discussions of the role of Western intellectuals between the two World Wars, whole nations have already been put at risk and indeed led into disaster, by a climate of opinion to which the intelligentsia have made major contributions. (Sowell 2006, p. 288)

For Sowell, then, intellectuals are totalitarians with influence over the young and impressionable. Nations are endangered by their meddling, and wars erupt because of their ideas.

Deficit of Power (s₂)

If Strauss, Aron, Johnson, Lilla, and Sowell alert us to the terrible dangers posed by intellectuals, their political counterparts within conservative discourse do not appear convinced that this is due to an excess of power. Indeed, politicians tend to employ exactly the opposite rhetoric, often depicting intellectuals as bizarre, effete, and useless to society at large. They contribute nothing of value to society and do not have much in common with the average person. Thus, at the other pole within this discourse, intellectuals appear to have little or no potency. This position, generally associated with conservative politicians, derides intellectuals as ineffectual and useless. In the 1960s William F. Buckley famously declared that he would "rather be governed by the first two thousand names in the Boston telephone directory than by the faculty of Harvard" (Robinson 2008).[9] The preference points to the inability or incompetence of the presumably educated faculty of Harvard to govern in relation to the presumably less-educated list of names randomly selected from the phone book.

Such sentiment is echoed in the context of more recent politics. In reference to anthropologists and other social scientists, Florida Governor Rick Scott recently declared their extraneousness to his state, saying, "we don't need them here" (Bender 2011). Indeed, Scott then declared the state ought to focus its resources on more practical pursuits in science, technology, and engineering, or, "Those types of degrees that when they get out of school, they can get a job" (ibid.). In effect, Scott's position is that certain pursuits— those pertaining to more intellectual activity—are less pragmatic because they are less likely to secure employment for their practitioners. Republican presidential candidate Herman Cain mocked the intellectualism of Barack Obama and, at a rally to hundreds of enthusiastic supporters, declared, "We need a leader, not a reader" (Peoples 2011). The essence of this claim is that genuine leadership is antithetical to intellectualism, or at least literacy. A leader is a person of action, not the mind or books. Leadership is decisive, not thoughtful or contemplative, as such men are likely to be dithering. Indeed, this perspective on the divide between political practice and intellectualism was expressed most poignantly in an interview between the author Ron Suskind and an anonymous official from the George W. Bush administration. Suskind writes:

> The aide said that guys like me were "in what we call the reality-based community," which he defined as people who "believe that solutions emerge from your judicious study of discernible reality." I nodded and murmured something about enlightenment principles and empiricism. He cut me off. "That's not the way the world really works anymore," he continued. "We're an empire now, and when we act, we create our own reality. And while you're studying that reality—judiciously as you will—we'll act again, creating other new realities, which you can study too, and that's how things will sort out. We're history's actors . . . and you, all of you, will be left to just study what we do. (Suskind 2004)"

One role is passive while the other is quite clearly active. In that sense, the intellectual merely studies, while the politician acts boldly, potently shaping the world in his image. The intellectual is so clearly enfeebled that she is wholly dependent on the virility of the political practitioner for her vocation. She is parasitic; her work is ancillary to the deeds of the efficacious politicians.

While Sarah Palin (2010, p. 210) laments the presence of an "influential academic and legal elite," it is also true for her that the vast majority of Americans oppose their views.[10] Newt Gingrich, a former academic and, more recently, congressman and presidential candidate, blamed a "snob effect" of corrupting academics on American decline (Connors 2011). Another presidential candidate, Mitt Romney, who would ultimately become the nominee of the Republican Party, in spite of his privileged upbringing, extraordinary wealth, and education at Harvard, asserted that his cabinet would "not be filled with academics and politicians alone," but with "people who have had 'real jobs'" (Bailey 2012). Notwithstanding the irresistible irony that Romney could easily be said to have never worked a real day in his life—by many standards of work—the implication is clear; academics lead lives of soft comfort that hinder their understanding of reality. While Romney appears to equate academics with politicians, there is a clear difference between the two categories. No one would mistake politicians for academics. Romney continued by stating he would incorporate individuals with "experience in the real world" and rely on the type of individual that "understands how the economy works" (ibid.). Presumably, this means that economists do not, despite their training and studies, understand how the economy works.

There is, then, a profound disparity between the anti-intellectual rhetoric of academics and politicians. For someone like Thomas Sowell, intellectuals maintain a certain expertise in their fields but pose a grave threat to society when they drift beyond the borders of their proper disciplines. In the view of anti-intellectual academics, intellectuals are supremely dangerous, owing to their propensity for meddling in affairs for which they have no business. Yet, for a politician like Mitt Romney, intellectuals are incompetent even in their areas of expertise. Such is the implication of Congressman Steve Stockman deriding the president as the "Law Professor-in-Chief" or Senator Scott Brown's clearly derogatory use of the term "professor" in labeling his opponent, Elizabeth Warren. An academic does not understand how the economy works. Such wisdom is gained only by working a "real job."

IN THE GUISE OF ORDINARY MEN

Although the academics and politicians express remarkably opposed views on the nature of intellectuals, they are not altogether different. Both views refer to the extent of *power* possessed by intellectuals, albeit in a contrary manner. For the anti-intellectual academics, intellectuals are decidedly dangerous. For the politicians, however, such figures are largely ineffectual. Indeed, for the latter intellectuals would seem to pose very little danger and ought to be dismissed as irrelevant. This dichotomy gestures toward the initial contrary seme within conservative anti-intellectual discourse. Both terms pertain to power, but whereas the academics represent intellectuals as harboring a dangerous *surplus of power* (s_1), the politicians depict a contrary account in which intellectuals manage a pathetic *deficit of power* (s_2).

A host of synonyms might accompany these broad semic terms. A surplus of power indicates a dangerous kind of person, one with an excess of potency. Moreover, this danger lurks in society as a kind of cancerous fifth column, destroying from the inside out. Inversely, the deficit of power, because

(surplus of power) s_1 $\longleftrightarrow$ s_2 (deficit of power)

Figure 3.5.

it refers back to the intellectual, indicates a category of pathetic impotency. Here the intellectual is essentially an incompetent waste, incapable of understanding practical concerns or even the subjects in which he or she is supposedly proficient.

It is worth reemphasizing here, as indicated by the evidence presented, the anti-intellectualism of conservative academics and politicians does not refer, in the strictest sense, to the activity or life of the mind. Importantly, it is a denigration of a category of people, an attack on *intellectuals as people*. The contradictory semes are generated from negations inherent to the contrary semes. In taking the first term, *the surplus of power* (s_1), the question becomes what kind of individual contradicts excessive power. What kind of individual does not pose a threat or represent dangerousness? As Thomas Hobbes (1996, p. 87) reminds us, every human being bears at least some potential for danger, and even the weakest can kill the strongest. Hence, the negation of this term points toward something less than human, the intellectual as *subhuman* ($\sim s_1$). Likewise, the negation of the deficit of power (s_2) indicates something that is neither irrelevant nor impotent, something not incompetent. It has been said that all human beings rise to the level of their own incompetency, but this sort of individual contradicts that; it is categorically *not* incompetent. Hence the negation of this term gestures toward something more than human, the intellectual as *superhuman* ($\sim s_2$).

These contradictory semes form a consistent relation with their corresponding contrary semes. Of course, a superhuman figure contradicts one with a deficit of power, which is the politician's representation of the intellectual. However, as it should, the superhuman forms a coherent relation with the conservative academic view in which the intellectual has too much power, too much influence, and could conceivably engender disaster. Likewise, the view of some politicians toward intellectuals is one of abjection and near disgust. The intellectual is irrelevant and impotent. It is a pathetic subhuman creature.

The original contrary semes, the surplus of power (s_1) and the deficit of power (s_2), also generate a synthetic position of privilege within the discourse, the complex term (S). That which lacks power has less relevance,

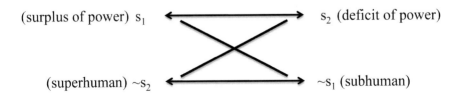

(surplus of power) s_1 s_2 (deficit of power)

(superhuman) $\sim s_2$ $\sim s_1$ (subhuman)

Figure 3.6.

while that which has excessive power is dangerous. The synthetic term suggests, in an almost Aristotelian sense, the proper balance between impotency and potency, between having so little power as to be less than human and having so much power as to be a danger to society. The complex term in this discourse consists of the proper kinds of power in the shape of the conservative individual (S). Virtuousness in this regard is the power to conserve the prevailing order. One cannot be powerless to defend the values, morality, and rationale of capitalism, nor should a desirable, virtuous individual possess the power to destroy it.

It is, however, the neutral term (~S) that is of the greatest priority here. The neutral term is the position that has been emptied of value, or, to reiterate Greimas's claim, a total absence of meaning.[11] In examining the contradictory semes of superhuman (~s$_2$) and subhuman (~s$_1$), it becomes apparent that they are unified in the neutral term by a common, synthetic feature. Both superhuman and subhuman are essentially perversions of what is properly human. Whether less than human, or more than human, both terms point to what is *other* than human. Hence, the neutral term, the term signifying privation as opposed to privilege, is undoubtedly *the inhuman* (~S). In that regard, the terms of conservative anti-intellectual discourse aim at the production of a representational structure in which the intellectual is inhuman. Regardless from which position it emanates, from the academic's fear of a superhuman danger or the politician's disgust for an impotent subhuman, the structure of conservative anti-intellectualism generates an image of the intellectual in which it is deprived of humanity, in which it is not human, a perverted distortion of human being.

While the neutral term, the object of privation, is identified with the inhuman, the complex or privileged term would, therefore, imply that which

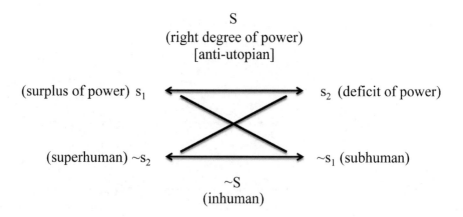

Figure 3.7.

is properly human as determined by the correct degree of power. The right degree or kind of power appears to be that which conserves the present system and deflects the corrupting dissent of the intellectual. For that reason, the complex term identifies the properly human with the anti-utopian (S).

Naturally, the question arises of what advantage is gained from representing the intellectual as inhuman. How does this structural effect serve the aim of counterrevolution? Here, I return to the humanist Marxism of Herbert Marcuse and his reminder that the strategies of counterrevolution rely on the subversion of reason. The representation of intellectuals as inhumans is not merely a function of language itself. Representation is an act and, indeed, the denigration of intellectuals by various academic and political figures detailed above constitutes a *deliberate* act. In that regard, the representation of intellectuals as inhuman is the product of a specific kind of action in which an object is reduced to inhumanity. These conservatives are responsible for *dehumanizing* intellectuals, for depicting them as more or less, but always other, than human. That is, by compromising the humanity of the intellectual in their various representations, these conservatives engage in a strategy of dehumanization.

Of course, these acts of dehumanization do not transpire merely for their own sake. They serve a larger, counterrevolutionary purpose. To represent the intellectual as inhuman is to dehumanize the intellectual. Once dehumanized, the artifacts and possessions of the intellectual become a kind of dehumanized property. The products of the intellectual, its work and ideas, its criticisms and values, are likewise dehumanized. The male "professor," as Cohen (2010) reminds us, is most discernible according to the stereotypically strange uniform in which he is garbed—tweed jacket and pipe.[12] This is the uniform of the professor, a visual indicator of bizarreness, and of course no normal person would wear such an outfit. However, the tactics of dehumanization have less to do with ridiculing the vestments of the intellectual than the source of her labors—reason. Most importantly, the medium of the intellectual, reason is transformed into a faculty belonging to the nonhuman. Reason becomes the tool par excellence of those who are alien. In this manner, the dehumanization of the intellectual, representing him or her as the inhuman, is instrumental toward the *alienation of reason*, a fundamental goal of the counterrevolution. Again, Marcuse alerts us to this central aim of counterrevolution, the total defamation of reason that transpires in both theory and practice. Dehumanizing those who use reason renders reason itself as a tool of that which is not human. Its use is regarded with suspicion and mistrust since those whose vocation involves reason are either dangerous superhumans or pathetic subhumans, but always inhuman.

THE WAY TO INHUMANITY

The structure of anti-intellectual discourse is symptomatic of the counterrevolution. That is, the diametric representations of intellectuals as either invested with extraordinary power, or weaklings divested of power, support the suppression of dissent. To dehumanize the intellectual is to subject the tools and products of his or her labor to dehumanization. Those objects and values that belong to the inhuman are associated with the nonhuman. Thus, the dehumanization of the intellectual serves to alienate reason. Especially in its critical formulation, reason thereby becomes something that ought to inspire wariness in the genuinely human. In the counterrevolution, reason is the way of the inhuman. In this manner, representing the intellectual as superhuman or subhuman is a crucial aspect of the counterrevolutionary subversion of reason. The dehumanization of the intellectual is pivotal in the neutralization of dissent. As its practitioners are relegated to suspicious aliens, political education is loses its efficacy through this practice.

As indicated by Aristophanes' *Clouds*, derogatory representations of the intellectual have a very long history. This begs the question as to whether or not the counterrevolution affected an ancient prejudice. It may very well be that these recent practices have imparted a special character to the maligning of intellectuals, or it may be the same as it has always been. Regardless, the point is that the structure of anti-intellectualism serves the aims of the counterrevolution as Herbert Marcuse describes them. In this counterrevolution, the alienation of reason serves the aim of neutralizing dissent and imagining alternative possibilities. It is decidedly anti-utopian.

In conservative discourse, the intellectual, and especially the academic, is represented as an inhuman. If the academic ought to be ridiculed, guarded against, then his or her authority is compromised to at least some degree. The decline of this authority raises the question as to what becomes of the university student when the professor is imputed with inhumanity. One might expect that as the authority and reputation of the academic declines, the status of the student, as the follower of the academic would follow. As I will show in the next chapter, this is not the case. Rather, the student replaces the academic, but only as a kind of perverse authority. Indeed, forces exogenous to the university encourage the student to understand himself and herself in a manner that is both contrary to the purposes of education, and useful to the functioning of capitalism: the consumer-student.

NOTES

1. One might argue that structuralism itself has received a very tepid reception within political science, finding rare instances of expression in a work such as Kenneth Waltz's

Theory of International Politics. While it is an acclaimed and essential text within the discipline, it still represents only a diluted attention to "structure."

2. Specifically, Strauss seems most concerned about the heterodoxy of the left, writing that Plato's presentation of communism in *The Republic* could not be taken as sincere because communism is "against nature" (Strauss 1964, 127). He makes this claim despite the fact that Plato was strongly influenced by the Pythagoreans, who "made their possessions available to the poor for common use" (Riedweg 2005, 112).

3. Strauss voiced opposition to a number of writers beyond the spectrum of the left, such as Machiavelli and Nietzsche. However, the brunt of his displeasure appears to be directed at those who would clearly be identified with the political left: Jean-Jacques Rousseau, Karl Marx, and Jean-Paul Sartre among others.

4. This peculiar verbiage is actually prevalent in Johnson's analyses. He spends quite a bit of time discussing the unusual shape of Jean-Jacques Rousseau's penis and urination habits, as well as the sexuality of several other figures. It never becomes clear if the shape of Rousseau's member is meant to offer insight into his thinking, or if bizarre sexual habits are simply a reason to discredit those with whom Johnson clearly disagrees.

5. It has been documented that Foucault was in favor of the overthrow of the Shah of Iran in 1979. His endorsement, however, of a popular uprising against a brutal dictator was not identical to extolling the virtues of the theocratic regime that followed.

6. Original emphasis.

7. Sowell appears unable to recognize the decidedly political components of linguistics and philosophy. One might ask whether or not this indicates ignorance on these subjects, and whether or not Sowell—an economist by training—was also commenting on subjects on which he had no business commenting.

8. Clearly, at this point Sowell has abandoned all pretext of assessing "intellectuals," which is little more than a thinly veiled façade for leftists.

9. The reader might reasonably question Buckley's inclusion in the category of politicians. Given that he ran, albeit unsuccessfully, for mayor of New York City, allegedly worked for the Central Intelligence Agency, promoted political activism, and was appointed delegate to the United Nations, he clearly engaged directly in the work of political practice eschewed by the academic critics of intellectualism.

10. It is not clear, given this vast opposition by "real America," as to whom the "influential" elite actually influences.

11. Again, referring back to Jameson's example, if the complex term indicates a spectrum of colors, then the neutral term would probably refer to colorlessness.

12. Even if this image is anachronistic, it remains a salient view.

Chapter Four

Degrees of Vulgarity

On the Reproduction of the Relations of Consumption in Higher Education

BURYING THE GRAVEDIGGERS

So far, I have examined how the counterrevolution is exercised through education policy, particularly in the exertion of state power over curriculum, aborting the faculties of reason before they can ever develop into criticism or dissent. In the service of this subversion, counterrevolution also strikes at those who promote the use of reason, the intellectuals and academics, portraying them as alternately superhuman or subhuman, but always inhuman. The effect is the dehumanization of the intellectual and the alienation of reason, a means to further neutralize political education. Now, I turn to consider how counterrevolution affects the primary instrument of ideology—the school, particularly at the apogee of higher education—to reformulate the ideological subject in late capitalism.

Curiously, as the intellectual sinks in representation, a peculiar figure of the college student rises. This is true at least insofar as the contributions of the intellectual are called into question while the student is increasingly the object of solicitation and pandering. This is facilitated by administrators eager to know above all else what the student desires and, when possible, to install certain kinds of desire. Thus, the ascension of the student does not occur on the basis of any intrinsic value or respect. The college student does not rise because he or she is cherished for any special knowledge or egalitarian sensibilities, but because he or she represents a scarce resource, a contested commodity in the competition between universities vying for precious funds. While the intellectual sinks, the student is valued by the institution and

51

the state in the same way as a private firm values a customer, as a consumer of products and services.

The decline in manufacturing and industrial jobs in the United States precipitated a fundamental shift in the nature of American capitalism. It might be observed that, historically, the United States had been most noteworthy for its industrial and manufacturing capabilities. We used to produce things. Now, we buy things. Indeed, we buy things most often made elsewhere. Of course, there is still manufacturing employment in the United States, but the material and ideological character of capitalism in this country now emphasizes consumption—purchasing objects, using them up, and then purchasing replacements in an unyielding cycle. This is consumer capitalism. Accordingly, I proceed from the premise that production has been surpassed by this logic of consumerism in which the false needs of the individual are supplied exogenously. As Marcuse observes:

> The people recognize themselves in their commodities; they find their soul in their automobile, hi-fi set, split-level home, kitchen equipment. The very mechanism which ties the individual to his society has changed, and social control is anchored in the new needs which it has produced. (Marcuse 1964, p. 9)

The recognition that Marcuse identifies as being integral to consumer capitalism demands the production and dissemination of a supporting ideology. Consumer capitalism could not succeed without consumerism, the ideology transmitting the logic of consumption. Just as Althusser explains that the reproduction of the relations of production occur by ideology, we can also expect the reproduction of the relations of consumption to occur according to that same principle. Hence, the school ought to play a central role in the reproduction of consumerism. As I will argue, the shift occurring within the scene of the university plays a most counterrevolutionary role.

While consumerism in general is not difficult to detect, it can be obscured on campus where it remains relatively subdued, at least when compared with the surrounding ostentatious society. The sheer volume and noise of the rest of society tends to overshadow the significant appearances of consumerism in the university. It is perhaps most easily detected in certain punctuated episodes, and, from there, traced back to more pervasive conditions. Though it is often encouraged and facilitated by administrators, the logic of the consumer has a tendency to run amok. Such were the recent cases of mass cheating at Harvard and the University of Central Florida. In terms of prestige and reputation, one could not find a more yawning chasm than that separating these institutions. Nevertheless, during the fall of 2010, nearly two hundred of the six hundred students enrolled in a business class at UCF were implicated in an attempt to share answers on a multiple-choice examination.

In the spring of 2011, about half of a nearly three hundred student political science course at Harvard came under investigation for sharing answers to a written examination. Cheating is not terribly remarkable, and we ought to avoid indulging in fabricated surprise that Ivy League students would stoop so low as to emulate a working-class school like UCF. Even the scale of the cheating is not terribly surprising. Rather, what ought to draw our attention is the attitude shared by a number of students interviewed after the scandals surfaced. In both cases, implicated students responded with indignity, protesting that purchasing answers and sharing them with others in the classes had been justified. In fact, at both universities many students took the position that it was the instructor's fault, either because he had made the course excessively onerous (as in the case of Harvard) or because the answers for the examination were available for purchase online (UCF). In effect, many students, whether they cheated or not, expressed a sense of entitlement; success in a course should be a function of either student preferences or purchases. Hence, the class should be less rigorous because that is what students want, and, if students wish to purchase answers from the Internet, that should not be considered academically dishonest. In effect, the attitude, which is generally pervasive, can be distilled to the idea that since the student paid for the course, the student ought to get what he or she wants as a result (presumably an 'A' as a final grade). This particular symptom of consumerism is not an aberration, and is instead an intensification of the otherwise prevailing conditions. It is merely the logic of the consumer carried beyond the point that administrators are prepared to encourage. As with the industrial forces of capitalism that accelerate the system to the point of crisis, they continue to encourage that logic, even if they cannot control it.

This shifting emphasis toward consumption raises a question. Again, Althusser (2001b, p. 105) tells us that the school creates ideological subjects, workers or managers, for the system. If the school serves the purpose of creating ideological subject, then it fulfills the aims of reproducing the relations of production. Toward that end, one would expect the school to create workers, given that capitalism thrives on parasitically extracting the surplus-value from the labor process. Yet, in Marxist theory, the creation of those workers, necessary as it is to the functioning of capitalism, is also supposedly catastrophic to the system. As Marx explains, by creating these exploited workers, capitalism also creates the future revolutionaries. This is one of several contradictions inherent to the capitalist mode of production. In order to profit, the bourgeoisie had to create a class of workers to exploit. Of course, in doing so, they created a revolutionary class that would ultimately be the demise of capitalism and, by extension, the bourgeoisie. For this reason, Marx and Engels noted that what capitalism creates above all else is its own gravediggers. How, then, is the university used to adjust and account for this systemic contradiction, to bury the gravediggers? How has counterrevolution modified the schools to adjust for this contradiction in late capitalism? While the school still promotes the production of workers, the emphasis at universities across the country has been placed on creating a decidedly nonrevolutionary subject—the consumer. That is, I suggest, that the production of ideological subjects as laborers has been overshadowed by the production of ideological subjects as consumers. If this is the case, what is gained, in terms of counterrevolutionary objectives, in the shift from interpellating workers to interpellating consumers? How does this emphasis on consumerism benefit the counterrevolution?

In the next section, I will more thoroughly expound upon Althusser's representation of the school as a producer of ideological subjects in relation to Marx and Engels's account of the contradictions within capitalism. Following that, I detail the various symptoms of consumerism in the contemporary university. Regardless of program or major, the university interpellates individuals with the demands of consumerism. As I will show, Marcuse identifies the tenets of consumerism as integral to the functioning of totalitarianism in late capitalism. Finally, how can we understand this turn to consumerism? I again call on Marcuse's theory of counterrevolution to offer an interpretation of this shift from emphasizing the production of workers to the production of consumers. I believe this shift is perfectly consistent with counterrevolution insofar as this relocation of emphasis moves away from the potentially collectivizing experience of work, with its attendant hazards of revolutionary consciousness, and toward the more individuating and, therefore, antirevolutionary tendencies of consumption.

EXHUMATIONS AND EXAMINATIONS

In the view of Louis Althusser, any society is organized according to the relations of production. Material objects and technology do not command a necessary social structure. The fact that a bulldozer exists does not mean that we must divide ourselves into operators, mechanics, foremen, and owners. Those divisions of labor do not naturally emanate from the machine, but are instead socially enforced. Material forces allow for the possibility of different relations. No arrangements follow necessarily from those materials, which is what permits the possibility of communism functioning through the same means of production as capitalism. The power that subscribes individuals into particular divisions of labor, and seduces them into wholeheartedly endorsing those arrangements as right and proper, is ideology. Hence, for Althusser, ideology serves to reproduce the relations of production. And, again, for Althusser, there is no more potent source of ideological interpellation in the present mode of production than the school. In the most general sense, the school produces ideological subjects of capitalism, subscribers to capitalist ideology.

Subjects do not remain generalized, and quickly find themselves in one of two positions. As Marx (1985, 80) pointed out, the competitive and exploitative nature of the system means that very few individuals can remain passive observers. One either owns some aspect of the means of production or becomes compelled to work for someone who does; one is either a capitalist or a worker (or on the way to becoming one). The school serves a preparatory role, or, as Althusser further explains:

> As an element of this process, the ISA's *contribute* to this reproduction. But the point of view of their contribution alone is still an abstract one. It is only within the processes of production and circulation that this reproduction is *realized*. It is realized by the mechanisms of those processes, in which the training of the workers is "completed," their posts assigned them, etc. (Althusser 2001b, p. 124)

Going to school does not confer the status of a worker. Rather, attending school merely designates individuals as students. But what the school does in this regard is to prepare the individual for their role as a worker. It is irrelevant whether that individual is a blue- or white- collar worker. The school prepares us, interpellates us, for these roles. Oftentimes, the school still resembles the factory model that it was designed to replicate and service. From secondary schools to higher education, vestiges of the assembly line are still visible. Students go from classroom to classroom, as they might traverse workstations. Chairs are often arranged in orderly rows resembling the assembly line itself, and there is most often a hierarchical arrangement that clearly delineates the students from their instructor, just as the foreman observes the labor of his workers. To this day, secondary schools often employ a bell, buzzer, or similar auditory signal indicating the beginning and ending of class, thus resembling the bell or whistle traditionally used to sound changes in the work shift. The quality of student work is inspected as the manager of an assembly line might judge, and reward or punish, employees.

And indeed, the demand of capitalism to produce a legion of workers persists. Universities are under pressure to divert resources from fields deemed less pragmatic and toward those in the areas of science, technology, engineering, and mathematics, the aforementioned STEM fields. The emphasis on producing workers in these fields is clear enough. Firstly, individuals trained in those areas are more readily exploitable in conjuring commodities than those engaged in more ephemeral fields such as the arts and humanities. Creativity may be important in a competitive marketplace, but only in conjuring new products and new avenues to profit. That is, creativity exploited by the system is desirable while creativity that subjects the system to criticism is extraneous. Secondly, the resourcing of science and technology ensures the production of more scientists, more technologists. A larger supply of such workers diffuses their individual value and bargaining power. As Marx tells us:

> On the basis of political economy itself, in its own words, we have shown that the worker sinks to the level of a commodity and becomes indeed the most wretched of commodities; that the wretchedness of the worker is in inverse proportion to the power and magnitude of his production. (Marx 1988, p. 69)

The larger the industrial platform and the more workers involved, the more meaningless each individual worker becomes. Each individual who rushes headlong into the scientific fields, lured by the promise of better wages and an easier life, a promise issued by the state apparatus and eagerly underwritten by its universities, helps undermine that interest. Nevertheless, it remains apparent that workers are still desired and that the capitalist state takes an active interest in their production.

However, the effort to use the Ideological State Apparatus, and in particular the school, to generate workers, whether unskilled, minimally skilled, or technologically advanced, is fraught with risk according to the Marxist view. Indeed, Marx observes that capitalism maintains a number of inherent contradictions that potentially threaten the system. Firstly, capitalism is predicated on the notion of private property and, therefore, the acquisition of private property. The process of acquisition meant that more and more property would eventually be concentrated in fewer and fewer hands, causing the system to contract violently (Marx 1985, 86). These cycles of accumulation and contraction are all too familiar as periods of growth or recessions and depressions. In combination with the other contradictions, this systemic flaw would eventually accelerate beyond control. Secondly, Marx observed that the capitalists depended on speed and efficiency for their profit. On one hand, the worker was pushed to the limits, and sometimes beyond, of human endurance. On the other hand, faster machinery was developed to gain a competitive edge. The same industrial machines that relegated the worker to obsolescence and created private property for the capitalist could also be harnessed toward more humane purposes in a communist mode of production. Hence, the technology that sustained capitalism, "the instruments of production," would make communism viable through a more rational utilization (ibid., p. 105). Instead of generating massive stores of military hardware, toupees, and useless trinkets, the same machinery would be made to address human needs and end poverty.

It was, however, another contradiction Marx observed that is most critical here. No matter how advanced the machinery has become, capitalism must have workers to exploit. Machines that replace workers on the assembly line still require technicians for maintenance and service. The dream of total automation has not yet been achieved. At the inception of capitalism, however, a veritable army of workers was needed, an intermediary of flesh between the capital of the factory machines and the final product. In fact, the bourgeoisie created the class of industrial workers to populate the factories and toil. But in creating the workers, the bourgeoisie created their nemeses. Unable to compete with the speed of the factory, more and more people found they had no alternative left but to find sustenance by working in a factory. As the cities swelled and the numbers of workers increased, the competition between capitalists intensified. With an abundant supply of workers, and a need to maximize profits, factory owners often paid their employees the smallest amount possible, the bare minimum needed to keep the worker alive in order to labor. Conditions were deplorable and safety was almost never a concern. Workers who were injured or maimed were no longer useful; they were replaced with any eager member of that always-expanding reserve army of the unemployed for whom the factory pittance was preferable to slow starvation.

The disparity between the dire conditions of the factory floor and the opulence of the bourgeoisie became apparent. Workers began to recognize the injustice of their situation and formed unions to augment their bargaining power and accomplish collectively what they could not individually. Gradually, and with great struggle, the working conditions of capitalism were sometimes improved, though never universally, and never completely. And indeed, the contradiction is never resolved. Capitalism needs workers that it can exploit. But, as Marx demonstrates, in creating those workers, capitalism creates a potentially revolutionary force. The deplorable circumstances of capitalist labor, the abject poverty the system invariably creates, and the unavoidable exploitation push the working-class, *the proletariat*, deeper into desperation until it has nothing left to lose.[1] The workers come to see themselves as sharing a common adversary. They unite. They unionize. They strike and sabotage the factories. Even workers who are enthralled by capitalism, those who would vigorously oppose any kind of collectivism, might adopt an adversarial posture with management and ownership in the effort to obtain greater benefits and pay. But the real danger for capitalism, Marx (1985, p. 90) noted, lies in the ever-expanding union of the workers, not in their specified industries, but as a *class* of workers. Regardless of their vocation, the proletariat class is exploited, and through that common, ignominious distinction, they could achieve solidarity and seize control. For this reason, Marx states that what capitalism produces above all other things, more than any other product, are the means for its own destruction. If so, the schools would seem to be supplying the shovels. If, as Althusser maintains, the school produces workers, then they are instrumental in creating the revolutionary class that will eventually destroy the system. Capitalism needs the workers to operate the means of production, but in creating those workers it potentially creates the future revolutionaries who will overthrow the system itself.

RATE MY OPPRESSOR

The contradiction of the proletariat poses a challenge for the production and dissemination of ideology. Creating workers is necessary, but it is also dangerous to the system. It threatens capitalism, even as it sustains capitalists. How have the schools, especially the institutions of higher education such as universities, mitigated this danger? Of course, the demand for workers is never eliminated, but factory work and manufacturing jobs have been exported well beyond the borders of the United States to regions where interfering labor laws and collective bargaining rights are far more favorable to the capitalist and the corporation. Workers are still needed, even in the centers of capital, but the emphasis has clearly shifted. Instead of endeavoring to produce a steady stream of future workers, the schools and universities are preparing a newer kind of entity for late capitalism—the consumer. Rather than stressing the training of individuals for the demands of the workplace, the emphasis has been resituated for preparing students to become consuming-subjects of the products of capitalism.

Practically every aspect of the collegiate experience is now designed to reinforce the centrality of consumption and naked, vulgar consumerism. For Althusser, one does not become a worker until one reaches a place of work. No one is a worker merely by the practice of attending a school, and, thus, the two arenas are always separated. Those who attend school are students; those who toil in the workplace are workers.[2] Now, it seems, the schools have managed to traverse that inconvenient barrier as the obstacle between marketplace and classroom has largely dissolved. In that regard, education is now always vocational, always practical, inasmuch as every student is necessarily a consumer. It truly is on-the-job-training, since the universal expectation, regardless of one's source of income, is to shop, purchase, and consume.

In late capitalism, the collegiate experience, ranging from admission to matriculation, imparts the imperative of consumption. Indeed, even prior to admission, the selection of a school is a shopping experience, one steeped in the dynamics of advertising as the institutions compete with one another for customers. Perhaps the premier authority in this stage of collegiate life is the annual publication of *U.S. News & World Report*'s "Best Colleges," which promises to rank more than 1,600 schools. Some schools, in an ironic reversal of circumstances, have fabricated data in order to earn a more favorable ranking. Like so many students, they cheat. Such was the case at Claremont McKenna College, which exaggerated "the collective SAT exam scores of incoming freshman classes for the last six years" in order to improve its attractiveness in the *U.S. News* ranking (Gordon 2012). Iona College, a Roman Catholic school, also inflated SAT scores "and high-school grade-point averages" of incoming freshmen in order to improve standings with a number of agencies "and entities that rank colleges, such as *U.S. News & World Report*" (Fuller 2011).

Less dramatically, the colleges and universities often employ advertising schemes and promotional rhetoric to entice potential consumers. A sample of these schemes demonstrates the recurring tropes of sating the desire for global command and imperialism. Universities promise the consumer will be "Worlds Ahead" as in the case of Florida International University. North Park University promotes itself as an institution where one can "Learn to Lead," while St. Edwards University advises its students to "Take on the World." Meanwhile, the University of Florida expresses the more or less totalitarian extent of consumer capitalism with its message to students that "The Gator Nation is Everywhere." It is coextensive with the world. Students at Oakland University, the University of Texas at Dallas, and the University of Toledo will be part of "Creating the Future." Beyond this vacant sloganeering, these institutions also advertise the quantitative variety of their catalogs. The University of Toledo claims to harbor "more than 200 student organizations" and "300 degree programs." Like most advertising, the promises are exceedingly vague. Students are not told just how they will actually create the future or why attending a university, or *this* university, is a better way to create the future. It seems fairly certain the future will be created regardless of which university one attends. Nor is it explained why one should find the purported ubiquity of the Gator Nation to be desirable. It seems unlikely that it is, in fact, "everywhere," and degrading to the value of the degree if it is true. Regardless of the questionable content embedded in these and similar advertisements, the effect of such schemes is to situate potential students as consumers before they ever set foot on campus. Buy the product and the rewards will be the power to create and command on a global scale. Even more moderate interpretations imply that a relationship exists between the purchase of a college education and a more desirable life. As many graduates are beginning to discover, the connection between obtaining a college degree and material prosperity is highly questionable. Before becoming admitted as a student, the individual is already enrolled into the ideological priority of consumption.

Of course, the process does not stop there. Instead, it only intensifies as the student is immersed in collegiate life. Here, most everything is arrayed for the benefit of the student-customer. In terms of the educational scheme, students literally shop for courses, majors, and degree programs from a catalog. Outwardly, it might seem that students labor rather than consume for their grades. Yet labor appears epiphenomenally, and the purchasing of a course often carries it with the expectation of a grade that appears satisfacto-ry to the consumer. That is, many students often indicate that because they paid for a course, they ought to receive a pleasing grade, usually the highest available. Paying for a class makes it "mine" to do with as I please, as is the case in any other purchase. And indeed, the world of higher education is filled with competitors. If my money is not welcome in one institution, if I cannot get what I want here, another will probably sell me the product I desire. In this regards, students who equate purchasing a class with purchas-ing a grade, or justify cheating as a form of consumer savvy, may understand what the universities are promoting better than the administrators and faculty who meekly, if ever, resist such attitudes.

The physical topography of higher education has also assumed the pos-ture of consumerism as well. Indeed, classrooms often still resemble factory assembly lines, but more than ever they also resemble the kind of vivid, image-saturated, spectacle of the market. The cost of higher education has risen dramatically over the last quarter century and this is in part due to the technological arms race universities have waged during that time. The desire to attract students with cutting-edge technology, or at least to avoid the appearance of lagging behind, has led "to increased spending on facility construction, especially lab and computer costs" (Odland 2012).[3] Every classroom must proudly and ostentatiously display the multimedia equip-ment, computers, projectors, and enormous screens that somehow indicate quality education. There is no resounding evidence to suggest that a Power-Point presentation improves learning or thinking, but to do without such expensive equipment in the classroom would be to place the institution at a comparative disadvantage in terms of luring customers. The prospective stu-dent learns from the universe of schools that he or she needs to be "worlds ahead" and responsible for the creation of the future in a technologically advanced classroom. Many institutions now accommodate space for fast-food restaurants and retail outlets. At the University of Central Florida, for example, there are vendors for eyeglasses, fraternity and sorority apparel, professional testing services, and thirteen fast-food restaurants in the student union alone. College campuses are now often host to shopping for university paraphernalia, pharmacies, video games, electronics, dry cleaners, beauty salons, banks, and more. There are often game rooms and entertainment centers, and, as in the rest of society, there are few places lacking a Starbucks coffee franchise.

If the line between university and shopping mall has become transparent, then it is more or less disintegrated by the presence of massive corporate entities vying for influence on campus. Corporate sponsors have eagerly stepped in to supply cash-starved universities with revenue, in exchange for advertising rights to the campus. At many institutions of higher education, the logos of Coca-Cola, Pepsi, Chevron, and others are readily visible, not merely as commercial adverts, but as sponsors of auditoriums, arenas, and buildings. At Florida International University, for example the Chevron logo festoons the building housing the School of International and Public Affairs. Coincidentally, the campus now hosts a "Global Energy Security Forum," which includes topics such as "Production of Unconventional Gas through Fracking" and "The Outlook for Energy: A View to 2030" delivered by an executive from ExxonMobil. Consulting firms abound for the purpose of guiding corporate entities how best to reach student-consumers and their money.

As semesters conclude, students are invited to register their opinions of courses and instructors. The process is not altogether different than how a customer might evaluate service at a restaurant. Satisfaction or dissatisfaction, contentment or discontent, can all be indicated on course evaluations. In effect, students are asked to report their experiences as consumers of a product. Unofficially, websites such as ratemyprofessors.com allow students not only the opportunity to register their views, but observe how others have assessed their instructors. Indeed, as one commentator writing under pseudonym at the *Chronicle of Higher Education* recently advised, all nontenured faculty ought to avoid irritating students and maintain a good reputation on websites such as ratemyprofessors.com. As the author explained, a college instructor who wishes to keep his or her job ought to identify discontented students, or at least those who might complain, and "make them all happier" (Pomerantz 2012). Whether this is hyperbole or not, employment decisions can be influenced by surveys and other instruments that measure student satisfaction. In this manner, students are interpellated as consumers by the institutions and instructors, and then demonstrate the successful dissemination of ideology by expressing levels of customer satisfaction or dissatisfaction with their purchases.

CONSUMER CONSCIOUSNESS

Marx noted that capitalism generates the workers who, once plunged into utter desperation, would have nothing to lose but the terms of their exploitation. The school, it appears, has responded in some measure to this contradiction. The requirement for creating work persists, but is buried beneath the primacy of consumption. Students may never become workers, but, by the fact of being students, they are always consumers. But how does the shift in emphasis from workers to consumers serve the interests of capitalism? How does it perpetuate class antagonisms to the benefit of those who own the means of production? My answer relies on tracing Marcuse's views on counterrevolution back to the works of Georg Lukacs, the Hungarian Marxist who is also sometimes considered the first discernible critical theorist. Lukacs explains that consciousness consists of two distinct and autonomous dimensions, the subjective and the objective. The subjective dimension of consciousness can be understood as the attitudes and preferences, the opinions and aspirations of an individual or group. The objective dimension refers to the actual conditions of reality. When an individual or group examines its conditions relative to the totality of society it stands a better chance of understanding those objective exigencies, and, crucially, when the subjective dimension of thoughts and attitudes is properly aligned with the objective circumstances, then true or *class consciousness* has been achieved. As Lukacs states:

> By relating consciousness to the whole of society it becomes possible to infer the thoughts and feelings which men would have in a particular situation if they were able to assess both it and the interests arising from it in their impact on immediate action and on the whole structure of society. That is to say, it would be possible to infer the thoughts and feelings appropriate to their objective situation. (Lukacs 1971, p. 51)

Under these circumstances, the subject, be it an individual or group or whole class, understands its actual circumstances and has corresponding views appropriate to those realities. For Lukacs, this meant that the working-class would recognize its actual, objective situation as exploited, but also as a potentially revolutionary force. By viewing itself in relation with the totality of society, the proletariat would see its role as both victim of bourgeois greed and instrument for the end of capitalism itself. In that sense, class consciousness is the first step toward the acquisition of revolutionary consciousness and a genuine revolution.

That step, however, appears elusive and the absence of revolution could be attributed to the lack of a developed class consciousness. Indeed, the workers, as Lukacs (ibid., 70) argued, the realization of class consciousness in practice was confronted with increasingly difficult obstacles. The subjective views and preferences of the workers were based on capitalist ideology that instilled untruths. The prevalent condition, then, was for the subjective dimension of consciousness to be misaligned with the actual objective conditions of reality (ibid., 50). Under this *false consciousness*, workers would cling to views that were not merely counterproductive; they might actually be harmful. Strikebreakers, for example, were almost always members of the working-class but would nevertheless undermine working-class interests on behalf of their capitalist masters. For a more recent example, there is a strong column of support for perennial presidential candidate Ron Paul on college campuses across the United States. Paul represents a mixture of libertarian views extolling the values of extraordinarily small government and moral conservatism (and occasionally racism) obscured under the convenient but thin façade of "states rights."[4] One of Paul's consistent campaign promises has been to eliminate the Department of Education and exercise the "smallest level of government possible" in supporting education.[5] Students at public universities and colleges where education is subsidized seem unable to appreciate that they support a candidate for president who would make it exceedingly difficult for them to attend college. In that sense, false consciousness means adhering to beliefs, values, and attitudes that are antithetical to one's own material interests.[6]

Despite the apparent proliferation of consumer choice, between universities as well as the myriad of options within them, the result is neither liberation nor freedom. For Marcuse (1964, p. 3), capitalism had become totalitarian precisely because of its tendency to implant and manipulate desire. Consumerism supports the permeation of totalitarianism in terms of supplying the individual with values and a false image of freedom. As Marcuse explains:

> Here, the so-called equalization of class distinctions reveals its ideological function. If the worker and his boss enjoy the same television program and visit the same resort places, if the typist is as attractively made up as the daughter of her employer, if the Negro owns a Cadillac, if they all read the same newspaper, then this assimilation indicates not the disappearance of classes, but the extent to which the needs and satisfactions that serve the preservation of the Establishment are shared by the underlying population. (Marcuse 1964, p. 8)

The point of consumerism is the *appearance* of freedom through consumption. The emphasis is merely to consume the false needs promoted and supplied by the system. From start to finish, college students are trained to practice consuming. This is not inherent to the experience of college, just as consumerism is not inherent to the experience of life. Rather, consumerism emphasizes the primacy of consumption as its own reward. The contemporary university includes far more activities of consumption than during any previous era. Colleges and universities did not always bear the signs of consumerism, just as general social conditions reflected different foci. Importantly, I am not suggesting that the educational apparatus no longer produces workers. Instead, my point is that the production of consumers has usurped the production of workers as the emphasis of the interpellation system. Regardless of which program or major or specialization one chooses, regardless of how advanced the degree one is pursuing, the education apparatus always imparts the imperative of consumption.

The shift in universities whereby the focus of interpellation has changed from generating workers to generating consumers serves the aims of counterrevolution, neutralizing the possible development of a revolutionary consciousness. It does so by guaranteeing the continuation of false consciousness insofar as it erects obstacles that prevent the formation of class consciousness. Work, especially in the industrial settings of capitalism, tends to be a collective experience. Even the stultifying, segmented work of the factory or the divisive office cubicle bears the possibilities of raising class consciousness. In the factory or office, *we* often work toward a common goal, whether it is collaboratively generating products or providing a service. Through the very process of work, a "we" can take shape. That is, workers can identify common interests through the shared experiences of their work. This is certainly not to suggest that all workers love one another or necessarily express solidarity. It merely demonstrates that one is more likely to have and recognize similar concerns with a co-worker on the assembly line or adjacent cubicle, than with the CEO.

Consumption, in contrast, is not often a collective experience. Rather, it tends to be an individual experience. Whereas the workplace can facilitate the recognition of class identity and interests, the focus on consumption amounts to a propensity toward individual concerns. In essence, the shift in education away from developing workers and toward developing consumers is consistent with the counterrevolutionary defamation of reason precisely because the individuating focus of consumerism is a diversion from revolutionary consciousness. Individuals are interpellated to emphasize consumption. Even the false promise of education leading to a better career is still only instrumental; the better career is not valued in itself but for the advantages it parlays as a consumer. A better job means buying better products and services. The shift toward emphasizing consumerism undermines the development of class consciousness in favor of an individuating consumer consciousness. In this manner, the dangerous contradiction within capitalism is deferred or postponed. Consumers are pliable clients of the system, whereas workers are potentially threatening adversaries. Consumers pose no threat to the Establishment. While it is true that they can form advocacy groups, the threat they represent is far smaller than even labor unions. A consumer boycott, for example, is necessarily limited to some fraction of the system, a corporation or, at most, industry. A union is predicated on the disparity in wealth and exploitative character of the system. While it may assume a mediating posture, there always lurks the potential for revolutionary consciousness within the union. Consumers are far more anodyne, and, in that regard, class consciousness is decidedly more threatening to the capitalist system than consumer consciousness.

Thus, under the conditions of the counterrevolution, the school has gone from being an essential institution for reproducing the relations of production to reproducing the relations of consumption. The school now emphasizes the centrality of consuming. In that regard, the school is a primary instrument of the counterrevolution insofar as it erects obstacles to the development of class consciousness. It preserves false consciousness by establishing consumer consciousness. Individuals still work and capitalism still produces workers. The development of a class consciousness remains a possibility, but this is constantly suppressed by the false consciousness arising from consumerism.

THE GOLD RULES

The counterrevolutionary subversion of reason transpires according to a number of tactics. First, while it appears as though the state is engaged in a debilitating assault on the school, its power is actually exercised toward detouring students away from areas in which revolutionary consciousness might develop. Concurrently, academic figures are demonized and dehumanized. This can have no other purpose than that of discrediting those who might facilitate the development of reason, criticism, and dissent. As Marcuse points out:

> Those who are educated have a commitment to use their knowledge to help men and women realize and enjoy their truly human capabilities. All authentic education is political education, and in a class society, political education is unthinkable without leadership, educated and tested in the theory and practice of radical opposition. (Marcuse 1969, p. 47)

Concomitant with the decline of intellectuals, academics and educators, the student is interpellated according to the conditions of consumer capitalism. This adjustment serves decidedly counterrevolutionary aims. Creating workers bears risks for capitalism insofar as those workers may develop a class consciousness according to the collective experience of labor. Consumer consciousness is predicated on individuation and egoism. Supplying the individual with false needs renders that person dependent on what the system can supply. In effect, the interpellation of students into consumers and the proliferation of consumer consciousness are tantamount to the production of a legion of counterrevolutionaries. Discussing the working-class, Marcuse (1969, 16) notes that while it may remain potentially revolutionary, "by virtue of its sharing the stabilizing needs of the system, it has become a conservative, even counterrevolutionary force." Strikebreakers are no longer a necessity when so many can be turned against their own interests. In this manner, counterrevolution preempts the development of class and revolutionary consciousness. The focus is turned from the possibility of recognizing a collective experience and injustice, and toward assuming the highly individualized posture of consumption. In the institutions of education, the signs of consumerism are ubiquitous not merely because of the encroachment of some exogenous ideology, but because the universities and colleges have themselves become instruments for generating consumers and, thus, mitigating the contradictions within capitalism.

As customers or clients, students expect expedient gratification. They are conditioned to respect the primacy of consuming. As Keith David's cynical character Frank explains in the science fiction film *They Live* (1988), "It's the "Golden Rule": He who has the gold makes the rules." Of course, if the student is being interpellated for these adjusted ends of consumerism, then, in the Marxist view, the material conditions of interpellation must have themselves been subject to modification. In the next chapter, I turn to consider how the counterrevolution is waged in an increasingly electronic classroom and claims a casualty in the art of teaching.

NOTES

1. While it may be argued that the proletariat refers exclusively to industrial, factory labor, Engels (1985, 79n1) describes the proletariat as "the class of modern wage-labourers who, having no means of production of their own, are reduced to selling their labour power in order to live." This is potentially a far more expansive definition and might just as easily include, for instance, hotel workers and office clerks.

2. Of course, those activities can transpire concurrently.

3. While Odland also identifies tenure as a problem, he points out that universities have tended to expand the ranks of administrators and bureaucrats while decreasing instructional faculty in both absolute terms and relative to the increased admissions of students.

4. Paul published a series of newsletters in the 1990s that claimed, for example, Martin Luther King, Jr. was a pedophile and that "95 percent of black males" in Washington, D.C. were criminals. It may not be the case that Paul wrote those letters himself, but it seems unlikely that he was unaware of what was included in publications with labels such as "Ron Paul's Political Report," "Ron Paul's Freedom Report," the "Ron Paul Survival Report," and the "Ron Paul Investment Letter" (Dougherty 2011).

5. These are statements taken from Ron Paul's website (www.ronpaul.com/on-the-issues/education/).

6. It is, of course, difficult to determine with any certainty just what constitutes objective material interests for an individual or class. For that reason, the idea of false consciousness might be dismissed as the arrogance of leftists using the authority of "objective conditions" to impose their views on others who simply disagree with them. One might easily ask why the Marxist does not suffer from false consciousness, why he or she understands the objective dimension of history more fully than anyone else. While I am receptive to these objections, they are too often the pretext for liberal or postmodern quietism. We may be wrong in diagnosing false consciousness in any given instance. That does not mean it exists nowhere. For that reason, I would prefer to be wrong and arrogant than ineffectively postmodern.

Chapter Five

The Art of Teaching in the Age of Electronic Reproduction

RECURSIVE ERROR

The emphasis on consumption, following from the alienation of reason and consumerist interpellation of the student, permeates the university. While workers are still produced by the Ideological State Apparatus, the focus of interpellation has shifted to consumerism because of its tendency toward individuation, rather than class consciousness. Althusser (2001b, 112) explains that ideology has a material existence, and, accordingly, we ought to expect a shift in the methods of education that correspond to the reorientation in interpellation. If a factory that had been producing television sets now manufactures computer monitors, then some change to the means of production has occurred. If the ideological product of education has changed, so must the material conditions under which education takes place. The logic of the consumer extends to the process of education, where the criterion of convenience prevails, serving counterrevolutionary aims.

Though it may run risk of appearing as nothing more than platitude, there is nevertheless an important assertion to be made about online teaching: it involves the use of computer technology. While that premise was admittedly unlikely to shatter anyone's conception of reality, it remains an inescapable condition, or perhaps affliction. Online classes always take place online, always involve the use of certain modes of technology, and, accordingly, always assume a specific form. Despite the apparent banality of these statements, in the present scene of counterrevolution, they are in no way innocuous. Rather, under the guise of transparently false egalitarian principles, the recent trend toward more online courses has the effect of imposing an aesthetic constraint on teaching. It should be uncontroversial, therefore, to proceed from the premise that technology matters.

It is one of the principle tenets of historical materialism that changes in the base of society will cause changes to its superstructure. The base consists of the material forces and available technologies at a given historical moment. Alternately, the superstructure is comprised of ideational forces: religion, politics, ideology, and so forth. In Marx's view, technology determines the possible content of ideas. As he writes in the preface to *A Contribution to the Critique of Political Economy*:

> At a certain stage of their development, the material forces of production in society come in conflict with the existing relations of production, or—what but a legal expression for the same thing—with the property relations within which they had been at work before. From forms of development of the forces of production these relations turn into their fetters. Then comes the period of social revolution. With the change of the economic foundation the entire immense superstructure is more or less rapidly transformed (Marx 1904, p. 12)

The implication of this observation is the reliance of ideas on the material conditions of social existence. As Marx (1998, p. 29) explains, "men have always formed wrong ideas about themselves," presuming the material world to be an instrument under their control. This false understanding is predicated on the notion that man's ideas determine the shape and content of his material existence. Yet, as Marx (ibid., p. 42) points out, this is completely backward given that "It is not consciousness that determines life, but life that determines consciousness."

Marx's writings on the relationship between base and superstructure were quite limited, having been restricted to a few words in *A Contribution to the Critique of Political Economy*, and then more or less assumed in *The Grundrisse* and the volumes of *Capital*. Accordingly, aspects of the interaction between these vital social forces remain opaque.[1] It was actually Walter Benjamin who first noted that the relationship between base and superstructure might very well be temporally asynchronous. While the material and technological forces of the base might advance with increased rapidity, the ideas of the superstructure might very well lag behind by decades. The effects of technological advancement on social consciousness would eventually become observable through their symptoms in the "areas of culture" (Benjamin 1968, p. 218). In that regard, art, literature, and music become indicators for how thought has been affected by the technological situation.

In Benjamin's view, art has been subjected to the vast machinery of mass production in capitalism. Though he notes that art had always been reproducible by artisans and apprentices of the great masters, the capitalist mode of reproduction was qualitatively different. Whereas reproduction in a Renaissance workshop was carried out by an aspirant or acolyte, but always by a human being, reproduction in capitalism was the result of a machine. Precisely because the human intermediary between original and reproduction had been excised, Benjamin (ibid., p. 220) tells us that "even the most perfect reproduction of a work of art is lacking in one element: its presence in space and time, its unique existence at the place where it happens to be." Every mechanical reproduction is an imposter, the work of a soulless machine that purloins the aura of the original as each copy is artlessly generated. Furthermore, the implements of mechanical reproduction find their apex in the production of film, an art form that, because it inherently involves the use of machinery (viz. cameras and sound equipment), automatically lacks aura.

Benjamin's primary concern, however, is not what has happened to art but the symptom art expresses. If, as Marx (1904, p. 11) states, "It is not the consciousness of men that determines their existence, but their social existence that determines their consciousness," then art, insofar as it is produced by the material conditions of society, can have a direct effect on consciousness. Benjamin (ibid., p. 234) affirms this, writing, "Mechanical reproduction of art changes the reaction of the masses toward art." Indeed, he notes that while art created under traditional conditions leaves open the possibility for thinking, mechanically reproduced art, such as film, imposes itself on the viewer who goes from active observer in the case of a theater to a passive witness in the case of a film. The massive proliferation of copied art leaves the viewer less able to appreciate the authenticity of originals. Likewise, the spectacle of film renders its audience passive, distracted, and entertained rather than enlightened. For Benjamin, the film easily mirrors the dynamic of fascism with the commanding spectacle of the screen supplying an object of fascination for a pliant, passive, mass audience.

How has teaching become symptomatic of changes in the base? If art reflected the degeneration of consciousness caused by changes in the base, then the incorporation of new technologies into the act of teaching should also reflect a subversion of consciousness. A crucial difference is, of course, that teaching under the conditions of late capitalism has not been mechanically reproduced. Rather, as with the recent emphasis on staging courses online, teaching has become electronically reproduced. To further narrow the scope of the question, how is online teaching symptomatic of counterrevolutionary strategy? In order to address this question, I will first situate teaching as bearing an artistic quality by first explicating Louis Althusser's materialist aesthetics and then examining the act of teaching according to those views. Following that, I will discuss the current trend toward online teaching, especially in the university environment. Lastly, I will discuss Marcuse's views on aesthetics and revolution. The emphasis toward online teaching represents a counterrevolutionary strategy in the realm of aesthetics. By narrowing the range of pedagogical aesthetics to a specific format, the possibilities for radical thought are thereby limited.

TEACHING: THE PERFORMATIVE SYNTHESIS OF SCIENCE AND ART

The question as to whether teaching constitutes an art or a science may belong to the category of perennial and irresolvable questions. It is probably unproductive to endeavor to affix it exclusively into one or the other. Rather, we ought to ask what potential there is for teaching to be an art (or a science). To the extent that teaching is or can be an art, it can then be determined what effect the technologies of electronic reproduction might engender. Teaching is a general category of instruction. Here, I consider the formal variety as it might be encountered in schools, broadly understood. In that general sense, teaching is action that ostensibly maintains the purpose of engendering education. The question of art, however, can be far more vexing precisely because while most things are not art, many things can be. An exhaustive account pertaining to the meaning of art would be Sisyphean, an endlessly pointless task. The question at hand is whether or not teaching is purely labor, or if it can be art according to a Marxist view. For that reason, I return to the views of Louis Althusser, precisely because he directly addresses the distinctive functional natures of art and science.

Althusser's commentary on the distinctions between art and science are largely confined to a short but nonetheless important document, "A Letter on Art in Reply to Andre Daspre." As the title suggests, Althusser is answering correspondence he received from Daspre, a critic who claimed, "art provides us with a kind of knowledge" (Ferretter 2006, p. 96).[2] In his response, Althusser explains that art is not ideology itself, but can be ideological. In that sense, art is the representation of extant ideological conditions. In fact, Althusser offers similar statements on philosophy when he states that it is an effect of class struggle at a given historical moment. Ideology, one might say, operates beforehand, producing the subject. It does so most effectively when it escapes detection. Art may serve the purpose of interpellation, but only after it has been created as an effect of ideology by a prior subject. As Althusser notes:

> Every work of art is born of a project both aesthetic and ideological. When it exists as a work of art it produces *as a work of art* (by the type of critique and knowledge it inaugurates with respect to the ideology it makes us see) an *ideological effect.*" (Althusser 2001d, p. 165)

Art is first an effect of ideology, and then a cause. While this argument may seem infinitely circular, it corresponds to the larger formulation on base and superstructure that is central to historical materialism.

Ultimately, the most fundamental difference between art and science pertains to the unique species of idea that each conveys. Althusser tells us that art is that which supplies imagery and impression. In distinction, science is that which transmits knowledge. The two techniques of truth are not radically opposed, but distinctive in their approaches. As he explains, "a peculiarity of art is to 'make us see,' 'make us perceive,' 'make us feel' something which alludes reality" (2001e, p. 152). Art, therefore, does not convey specific propositions, which is the dominion of science. Art reflects the conditions of those propositions. Thus, the depiction of, for example, anti-union legislation in the context of class struggle would not constitute a work of art in Althusser's view. Such a straightforward analysis rests on directly addressing ideological content within the context of history. Alternately, using the elements of anti-union legislation in a story that illustrates the anomie of late capitalism would be art according to this view. Art, Althusser (ibid., p. 152) explains, is in a relationship "of difference" with knowledge. Rather than being opposed to knowledge, art reflects the experiential dimension of knowledge. As Althusser writes:

> What art makes us *see*, and therefore gives to us in the form of *"seeing,"* *"perceiving"* and *"feeling"* (which is not the form of *knowing*), is the *ideology* from which it is born, in which it bathes, from which it detaches itself as art, and which it *alludes*. (ibid. 152)

Works of "science explain the nature and function of ideologies" whereas "art provides us with a critical view of the ideologies" (Ferretter 2006, pp. 96–97). Accordingly, a biology textbook, while certainly an effect of ideology, primarily attempts to dispense a certain mode of knowledge. A satire of biology textbooks succeeds through parodying the underlying bases for biology or the use of textbooks. Whether explicitly or not, intentionally or not, for critical purposes or not, the satire—and indeed, all art—dredges up the ideological conditions of the scientific.

Implicit to Althusser's aesthetic theory is the fundamentally performative nature of art. In that regard, art is what art does. The rhetoric of Althusser's aesthetics consistently depicts action. Art "gives." Art "makes us see," "makes us feel," "makes us perceive." And, just as art performs certain functions, art is also performed. This is not to say that art, for Althusser, is subject to the intention of the author. Indeed, as he notes, authorial intentions are utterly irrelevant, "for at issue here is the play's latent structure and nothing else" (Althusser 1996, p. 141). The internal logic is constituted by the various relationships within the work of art. And whether in the form of a novel, play, or some other work of art, this logic is never the result of the artists' "agency." This emphasis on structure, however, does not diminish the performative component of art, which is fundamentally an expression of labor. As Althusser notes, "The play is really the production of a new spectator, an actor who starts where the performance ends, who only starts so as to complete it, but in life" (ibid., p. 151). In this view, the performance "can very well demonstrate the conditions of change and act as vanguard in the instigation of efforts toward transformation" (Kowsar 1983, p. 469). Thus, in Althusser's aesthetics, art is the result of performance in which the conditions of ideology are elucidated, which in turn potentially transforms spectator into performer beyond the confines of the theater. The spectator-become-performer then "makes visible" the conditions of ideology in the world-at-large.

Using Althusser's views, I suggest that teaching can be, in large measure, constituted by art. Importantly, this is not a necessary condition for any kind of instruction, which can certainly proceed in an artless fashion. Teaching, however, is a unique species of instruction. Thus, it is artistic, and when deprived of that vital component lapses into an artless instruction, which, as I will discuss in greater detail later, ought to be avoided. Understood structurally, teaching is an effect of the relationship between science and art brought into performance.

According to Althusser's criterion, teaching can be scientific. In that sense, it can transmit knowledge (assuming such a thing exists at its highest standards) and disseminate direct propositions pertaining to some depiction of reality. Indeed, it would seem to be an explicit function of teaching to convey at least some fact as part of the process of education. If it were devoid of any scientific element, if it dispensed completely with the transmission of facts, the activity would no longer be teaching and would instead be pure art. Concomitantly, instruction lacking any sensibility for conveying the conditions beyond knowledge, a mode of instruction purely devoted to knowledge, could also not be teaching and would instead be science. Teaching can also be artistic insofar as it projects something other than knowledge. Beyond merely pointing to whatever facts there may be, teaching explicates the conditions pursuant to those facts. Whether in the service of ideological interpellation, or as part of Leninist political education, teaching goes beyond the sterile dispensation of knowledge and incorporates the element of spectacle. This is true of a teaching in education, as it is teaching a social science. The fact of civil or electrical engineering reflects, if only on an implicit level, the social conditions in which the construction of bridges or power plants occur. Of course, the artistic aspect might be conservative; those extant social conditions might be lauded rather than criticized. Furthermore, the artistic component is not necessarily equal across disciplines and instructors.

Knowledge and perception are both present in the act of teaching. The classroom is not merely presented with fact, but the means for perceiving, feeling, and *seeing* the conditions of fact. In this regard, teaching is always performative. It is the synthetic performance of science and art. The science class involves at least a modicum of performance in order to explicate the conditions of scientism. Even the pretense of maintaining "objectivity" demands an articulation of positivist ideology. Likewise, the art class, at a minimum, depends on some principles for instruction. Teaching, therefore, brings together the elements of art and science through performance. In the present age of counterrevolution, where science is privileged to the detriment of art, teaching, which is constituted by an artistic component, is threatened by the imposition of a specific form of electronic reproduction.

COUNTERREVOLUTION 2.0

Debates over the merits of online education continue largely unabated and vigorous. Proponents argue that online courses and degrees permit access to students who would otherwise be unable to obtain education. Moreover, they argue that the costs to the host institution and the state, if the institution is publicly funded, are considerably less than in-person instruction. Opponents counter that online courses are qualitatively inferior and undermine the historic rationale of a university education. Some have noted, for instance, studies concluding that students enrolled in online courses suffer in terms of performance (Jaggars Smith and Xu 2010, 1; Jaggars Smith and Xu 2011, p. 1). Others insist that online learning "is quite literally the only option" for students who "would have no other way of enhancing their skills or seeking a degree" (Bacow, et al. 2012, 10n7).

Although these debates are important, my intervention does not pertain to the outcome of online education with regards to its efficacy or efficiency. Rather, my aim is to address the effects of online education *on teaching*. In order to do that, it is necessary to establish what is meant by "online education" in the first place. As Bowen, et al. (2012, p. 7) state, online learning "comes in a dizzying variety of flavors" and is "hardly one thing." From my perspective, that may constitute a serious and potentially hazardous overstatement.

The incorporation of the Internet into secondary and higher education essentially trifurcated courses into three different types: traditional, hybridized, and online.[3] A traditional course involves "no online technology" and would typically involve lecturing or discussion between an instructor and students in the presence of one another (Allen and Seaman 2011, p. 7). This mode of instruction requires either a classroom or similar physical (as opposed to virtual) meeting place. A hybridized course "blends online and face-to-face delivery" (ibid., p. 7). Some combination of personal instruction would be synthesized with the use of online teaching. The latter might consist of video lectures hosted on a website, virtual classrooms where lectures and discussions proceed in "real time," networked messaging systems, or even "highly sophisticated interactive learning systems that use cognitive tutors" (Bowen et al. 2012, p. 7). In a hybrid course, some or all of these tools are integrated into a format that would also include a component of traditional instruction. Online courses, however, involve instruction "where most or all of the content is delivered online" and "typically have no face-to-face meetings" (Allen and Seaman 2011, p. 7). Henceforth, where the term "online" is used as a modifier in describing teaching, education, or courses, I refer to a mode of instruction that transpires exclusively via electronic means.

Online courses can represent a considerable cost savings to universities, though not necessarily to students. One study indicated an institutional cost savings of between \$31 and \$105 "per student" (Bishop 2006). For the institution, online learning means being able to host more classes and students without the need for corresponding physical structures, such as buildings and classrooms. Moreover, the institutions can save money because there is virtually no limit to the number of students that can be enrolled in a course. In effect, online courses become a means to accommodate ever-larger classes, and transcend the limitations of physical classrooms. As Bowen et al. notes:

> In this hypothetical model, a full-time faculty member (usually a tenure-track professor) will be responsible for overseeing all sections of a large introductory course. The professor will be the faculty member of record for the class, and will be ultimately responsible for all academic aspects of the class (syllabus, exams, grading, etc.). Of course other instructors will assist with the actual implementation of tasks such as writing and grading exams—though in time we expect much grading to be done automatically (Bowen et al. 2012, p. 38)

Though promisingly cost-effective, the savings represented by online learning is not necessarily shared by the students. Tuition, on average, is the same for on-campus and online courses. While some institutions offer a modest discount for online courses, others impose a noticeable premium in the form of a "convenience fee." There is a savings opportunity for students in terms of ancillary expenses. Taking an online course means that one need not worry about the expense of transportation or parking, unless of course that student is also taking traditional or hybrid courses. Those costs are eliminated if a student enrolled is in an exclusively online degree program. However, a compatible computer with adequate Internet connection will be required, which are costs that may exceed parking and gasoline, or public transportation.

At present, online learning represents a significant presence in higher education. In 2010 more than six million students were reported to have taken at least one online class (Allen and Seaman 2011, p. 11). That number comprises more than 31 percent of students enrolled in American universities (ibid.). Furthermore, as Parker, Lenhart, and Moore (2011, p. 9) state, "Of the 1,055 college and university presidents interviewed for the Pew Research survey, 77 percent reported that their institution offers courses for which the instruction takes places exclusively in an online environment." In addition to courses taught online, there are now entire degree programs at both the undergraduate and graduate levels hosted exclusively online. Nearly 60 percent of those institutions where online courses are offered also "grant degrees for which all the course work can be completed online" (Parker, Lenhart, and Moore 2011, p. 4). In essence, these programs permit students to obtain university degrees, conceivably without ever stepping foot onto a university campus. While online baccalaureate and master's degrees are already quite common, online doctoral degrees are becoming more frequent. And, as Parker et al. (2011, p. 7) report, "Among college graduates who have taken a class online, 15 percent have earned a degree entirely online." These online courses and degrees are offered at all manner of universities and colleges. Whether community colleges or four-year schools, liberal arts colleges or research universities, public, private, or for-profit institutions, the vast majority are now offering online courses and degrees.

The trend toward more online education is expected to increase at institutions of higher education as well as primary and secondary schools. At present, over 30 percent of current students report having taken an online course, and Parket et al. (2011, p. 10) report the expectation from at least half of college presidents surveyed that "a majority of their undergraduate students will be taking a class online" within the next ten years. This appears to be consistent with the trend over the past decade. Between 2002 and 2010, enrollment in online courses increased from 9.6 percent of total enrollment to the present figure of 31.3 percent (Allen and Seaman p. 11). Some aver that online teaching will eventually eclipse the traditional form altogether and "face-to-face higher education will become a privilege of a few" (Parry 2010). This is not due solely to the demand of students and responsive institutions. Political power is being exerted in order to promote online teaching, not merely at the level of higher education, but in primary and secondary schools as well. A recent Florida law mandates all high school students "to have at least one online class before they graduate" (Flannery 2011). The Florida law is hardly novel, joining similar requirements by "Michigan, Idaho, Indiana, New Mexico, and Alabama (Flannery 2011). Additionally, a "Florida Virtual School," which provides kindergarten through high school education online, will begin awarding diplomas in 2013 (Flannery 2011).

From this data, it is readily observable that online teaching already represents a significant presence in college education. Moreover, these courses are expected to continue increasing. Beyond the college environment, online teaching is beginning to permeate secondary education, and, one wonders, when this format will infiltrate even primary schools. Of course, the problem is not in the technology itself, but in the fact that, like any technology, it is combined with power. Resources expended toward online courses are necessarily drawn from other areas. Expertise with online systems is now a requirement for many faculty positions, and some faculty members are now required to teach online courses exclusively. While some instructors have eagerly embraced these formats, it seems clear that this trend is the result of a deliberate campaign on the part of state governments and university administrators. To at least some degree, then, online teaching is imposed rather than chosen, and to that degree it is the result of coercion and power.

THE RESISTANCE OF FORM

The idea that online courses are less expensive for the institution is dubious. By all accounts, such formats actually appear more expensive for the student. Whether or not a student can obtain an experience in an online course equivalent to the one they might receive in a traditional, or even hybridized, format is quite contestable. Likewise, the notion that online courses can provide historically, geographically, and economically disadvantaged populations access to college education seems particularly questionable. After all, universities still seem to be in the habit of charging money for their degrees and credit-earning courses, and, if the grim prognostication that traditional courses will become the privilege of the wealthy becomes true, then the introduction of online learning may be nothing more than the harbinger of a de facto segregation.

Hopefully those questions will continue to be debated, despite the seemingly inevitable trend toward the proliferation of online courses and degrees. This project remains focused, however, on another question: what is the effect of online courses on teaching itself? To this point, I have argued that teaching can be understood as bearing an artistic quality according the aesthetics of Louis Althusser. How do the means of electronic reproduction affect the art of teaching, and, by extension, the possible modes of consciousness that follow? How does online teaching effectively serve the aims of counterrevolution? In order to address this question, I return to Herbert Marcuse, specifically his views on the political potential of art.

This potential originates with the phylogenetic composition of social life. Civilization arises at the cost of repression. The individual sacrifices some desire for pleasure in order to secure the advantages of cooperation. Scarcity and survival are more easily dealt with through combined efforts than they are by the exertions of an individual. The renunciation of desire, in the form of repression, meant that survival was earned at the cost of an increasingly assertive, even totalitarian, civilization. Marcuse (1964, p. 12) lamented the collapse in late capitalism toward one-dimensional thinking, wherein any thought beyond "the established universe of discourse" was easily repelled by the system. Instead, the individual is expected to conform to the "performance principle," which is the character of repression—its specific rules and order—during a given historical era. Whereas repression indicates restraints against *Eros* that may be necessary for survival, the performance principle reflects "the origins and the growth of this civilization" (Marcuse 1955, p. 44). In that sense, the performance principle points to political and social regimes that govern our daily lives. This occurs most clearly in the conditions of estranged labor, but "alienation and regimentation spread into the free time" (ibid., p. 47).

However, repression effectively splits the psyche into conscious and unconscious levels. Desire is repressed at the conscious level, but circulates in the unconscious. And while these mental realms are split, they remain linked through fantasy (ibid., p. 140). Hence, occasional expressions of the unconscious make their way into conscious activity, and, as Marcuse notes, the supreme example of this is located in art (ibid.). Because the unconscious exceeds the constraints of the performance principle, it is the unconscious, not the conscious, that is the seat of freedom. As he explains:

> Art, as an instrument of opposition, depends on the alienating force of the aesthetic creation: on its power to remain strange, antagonistic, transcendent to normalcy and, at the same time, being the reservoirs of man's suppressed needs, faculties and desires, to remain more real than the reality of normalcy. (Marcuse 1998, 202)

For that reason, Marcuse maintained that promise for radical action persisted in the crucial area of art. While he had some misgivings about the contemporary fusion of art and aggression, his aesthetic theory rested on the notion that any true work of art "provides the audience with the hint of a repressed happiness" (Bronner 1994, p. 244). Precisely because art can be the expression of unconscious freedom imported into the conscious world, it bears the possibility for resistance. Of course, art is practiced consciously and does not entirely escape the demands of the performance principle. A new form will quickly become appropriated by capitalism and converted into a commodity, an insipid palliative for consumption by the masses. Initially at least, authentic art is regarded as dangerous and subversive. The histories of early rock and roll, and hip-hop, attest to this threatening character. Novel art forms are unsettling until they are, almost inevitably appropriated and converted into an analgesic commodity. Nevertheless, as Marcuse (1978, p. 41) notes, "In this sense art is inevitably part of that which is and only as part of that which is does it speak against that which is." Of course, art is not fully free, but because it is linked to the unconscious via fantasy at least one crucial component of art can represent liberation.

Importantly, Marcuse is clear in showing us that what supplies art with its revolutionary potency is not the content, but rather the form. The content, in terms of meaning and message, pertains to the given reality. Instead, it is through the manifold possibilities of form that art can become revolutionary. As he explains:

> The content as such is irrelevant, can be everything (for everything is today the object of totalitarian domination and therefore of liberation) but it must be shaped in such a manner that it reveals the negative system in its totality and, at the same time, the absolute necessity of liberation. (Marcuse 1998, 203)

In other words, whatever is reflected in art is necessarily going to be an image of the unjust and oppressive social conditions. Thus, for Marcuse, the radical potential of art is not in its ability to reflect reality, but "in its power to break the monopoly of established reality (i.e., of those who established it) to *define* what is *real*" (Marcuse 1978, p. 9). Form, accordingly, becomes crucial as the means to displace the accepted view. Art is polymorphous, and, as an expression of unconscious freedom, uses form to transgress the established law.

Therefore, according to Marcuse's views, the plurality of possible forms is what supplies art with its revolutionary potential. It is in the ability to challenge the given conventions that art compels its audience to think in a different way, to defy the tendency toward one-dimensional thought, and open the possibility of breaking with conformity. As Marcuse (ibid., p. 32) writes, "Art cannot change the world, but it can contribute to changing the consciousness and drives of the men and women who could change the world."[4] Effectively, art is a visible symptom of the unconscious and the lost freedom buried by extraneous social demands. Regardless of the content, the meaning and message, art harbors this capability for provoking radical thought through the projection of different and defiant forms.

And this is precisely what is threatened by the imposition of online teaching. Again, Bowen (2012, p. 7) tells us that online learning cannot be considered one monolithic practice, and they are correct insofar as there are many tools that one can employ in the service of online teaching. However, this view is also dangerously misleading. There is one thing that is true of all online teaching in all circumstances, one thing that gives the entire category any semblance of coherence, without which "online teaching" would mean nothing. And while recapitulating this point may seem to be redundant and tautological, I suggest it is terribly consequential: online teaching always happens online. Regardless of what tools are employed in its service, the uniformly online nature of online teaching is what supplies its peculiar character, its aesthetic form.

Online teaching can never be anything but online. "Traditional" teaching is merely a name that was assigned a posteriori, as an after-effect of online teaching, and, ultimately, the differences between "traditional" and "hybrid" courses are forced.[5] Traditional teaching can make use of whatever technologies are available, or eschew them altogether. Online teaching must, by virtue of institutional design and rules, happen online. It is restricted to a certain format, and this restriction is often a function of power exerted by the state and its administrative subordinates. Students cannot, in an online course, be compelled to show up to an in-person classroom (that would be the purview of a categorically different kind of course). So, while traditional and hybrid courses maintain an array of aesthetic forms at their disposal (classroom, online, indoor, outdoor, etc.), the online course has just one—it must always be online. It can appear in no other form than through the means of electronic reproduction.

The expanding trend of online learning threatens the artistic, and therefore revolutionary, potential of teaching. As more teaching is converted to online, more teaching becomes aesthetically limited in its form. Consequently, the artistic potential of teaching is severely compromised, and, along with it, the possibilities for expanding thought in education. The more the form of art is limited, the less able it is to challenge the Establishment values. As Marcuse notes:

> The critical function of art, its contribution to the struggle for liberation, resides in the aesthetic form. A work of art is authentic or true not by virtue of its content (i.e. the "correct" representation of social conditions), nor by its "pure" form, but by the content having become form. (Marcuse 1978, 8)

Therefore, the conditions of electronic reproduction most acutely threaten the plurality of forms teaching can take, thus undermining the potential of form in provoking anti-Establishment thought.

AGAINST THE FUTURE

The danger of electronic reproduction lies in the threat to the political potential of art that Marcuse hails as the possibility for revolutionary thinking. As part of the superstructure, the work of art is transformed by changes in the technological and material base.[6] For Althusser, art is that which depicts the conditions of ideology, rather than conveying knowledge, which is the dominion of science. Teaching is the structural effect of art and science derived through performance. It can effectively accommodate both the artistic—making us see social circumstances—and the scientific—conferring direct propositions—within its presentations. As art, it becomes subject to the transformations in the base. For Marcuse, art maintains a revolutionary potential in its ability to express the unconscious through different forms. The conditions of electronic reproduction, specifically online learning, threaten the artistic component of teaching by limiting aesthetic expression to just one form—the online. Regardless of the tools employed, online instruction always deploys this limited electronic aesthetic. This serves the aims of counterrevolution inasmuch as the limitation of form restricts the artistic possibilities, and thus the potential to provoke radical thought. Therefore, I submit that the present political effort emphasizing online teaching is counterrevolutionary, whether deliberate or otherwise.

By limiting the possible aesthetic forms, electronic reproduction (viz. online teaching) threatens the very possibility of teaching as art, reducing it to mere science. In a dual sense, this serves the aims of counterrevolution. Firstly, the possibility of critical or revolutionary thought is severely impeded by a narrowing of aesthetic forms. Secondly, because the form of teaching is restricted to an electronic aesthetic, it loses its resemblance to art. Instead, the artless instruction that remains is able to convey ideas under increasingly restricted conditions. It assumes a stronger resemblance to what Althusser calls "science" than it does art. In that regard, the push toward more online teaching is perfectly consistent with the counterrevolutionary aim of conveying technical knowledge and scientific fact over assessing social concerns.

Neither this project, nor its author, can be correctly understood as standing in opposition to the use of electronic technology in teaching. In that regard, I am not hostile to online teaching or the utilization of the Internet in primary, secondary, or higher education. There is always some measure of promise or reason to hope, as Lukes (1994, p. 228) suggests, that with every new advent "technology is moving away from narcotic, ascetic, and elitist postures." Still, no science, technology, or tool emerges beyond the present system of power. As Marcuse notes, it is absurd to blame technology, which will ultimately be the source of liberation. He asks:

> Is it still necessary to repeat that science and technology are the great vehicles
> of liberation, and that is only their use and restriction in the repressive society
> which makes them into vehicles of domination? (Marcuse 1969, p. 12)

My aim here is to alert us to the use of technology that affects the practice of education according to the principles of counterrevolutionary power. The narrowing of the aesthetic dimension in the art of teaching does not serve the interests of education; it serves the interests of the Establishment. Hence, the claim that online teaching reaches more people is, from this perspective, not merely meaningless, but detrimental. Reaching more people in order to better prepare them for technical, artless, uncritical indoctrination in a system of estranged labor seems counterproductive and counterrevolutionary.[7]

Did the online aesthetic represent a new, and thought-provoking form when it was introduced? Perhaps, but it was quickly appropriated by a state apparatus concerned with efficiency and conformity. The problem is not the tool, but how it is used. Indeed, if the radical nature of art is located in its ability to radicalize thought through experimentation and innovation in form, then I would readily admit that the tools of electronic reproduction most certainly have a place in education. But those tools have to be subject to the manifestations of the unconscious, and not the calculus of efficiency as determined by a politician or administrator. If, as Marcuse (1955, p. 149) suggests, fantasy is the bridge between unconscious freedom and the products of consciousness, then the art of teaching ought to proceed according to the tenets of fantasy. Under the present conditions of estranged labor, that does seem rather unlikely.

It may be argued that online teaching has certainly not eclipsed in-person instruction. My response, derived from gesturing back to the observable trend (agreed upon by both opponents and proponents of this phenomenon), strongly indicating continued expansion of this format, would be: not yet. As one of my colleagues described the trend toward online courses and degrees, "That train has left the station." If so, we should dynamite the tracks. Of course, this technology renders education at least potentially accessible to working people or those who might otherwise be physically unable to attend college. But the percentage of courses offered electronically betrays that ideal. The motivation is money; the effect is counterrevolutionary. As of now, the fraction of education currently conducted online is alarming. Yet the more troubling point is that the rapidly expanding share of the teaching market appropriated by online education further threatens the development of radical thought.

NOTES

1. For instance, it seems unclear as to how the base changes at all if it is unaffected by social consciousness.

2. Althusser's response evokes the classic differentiation between art and science first articulated by Aristotle in his *Nicomachean Ethics*. Science, he claims, "is a state of capacity to demonstrate," while "art is concerned with coming into being" (Aristotle 1998, 141).

3. Allen and Seaman (2011, 7) identify four types: traditional, web facilitated, hybrid, and online. However, the distinction between web facilitated and hybrid is nominal, and, for the purposes of this project, web facilitated is subsumed under the category of hybrid.

4. There seems to be considerable agreement on this point between Marcuse and Althusser.

5. The label "traditional" seems intended to evoke something charmingly quaint, if not archaic and obsolete.

6. While Benjamin first forwards this assertion, Marcuse (1978, 1) concurs.

7. A more decidedly structuralist Marxist attitude might differ and suggest that augmenting the misery of the working class is a necessary condition for revolution. On that point, I am essentially agnostic.

Chapter Six

The Forbidden Library

Counterrevolution and the Political Obscene

THE FUTURE WE HAVE SEEN BEFORE

If there is a supreme example of this burgeoning synthesis between the logic of consumption and the electronic reproduction of teaching in the age of counterrevolution, it is surely the Massive Open Online Course, or MOOC. Developed as a means by which lecturers could simultaneously reach huge audiences, a MOOC would be conducted by an instructor addressing a potentially unlimited number of students through an Internet forum. No single meeting place or auditorium is required; students can access the course from wherever they have access to a computer. At the end of the course, students would be assessed via electronic testing, presumably in the form of a multiple-choice examination, in order to provide an assessment on what they had learned. The advantage of a MOOC lies in what it represents to a casual learner, someone who wants to learn about an interesting topic on his or her own time without the hassle and expense of dealing with an actual college course. A student can take a MOOC hosted by an instructor who would probably be otherwise inaccessible. Thus, thousands of students can learn a subject (even if it earns no official credit) from a teacher at Stanford or MIT, schools with very selective admissions standards. At the moment, most on-line mass-student courses have yet to be integrated into any certified degree program. The majority of students in a MOOC cannot obtain a degree or even degree-earning credit in this manner. Predictably, that seems very likely to change.

As an ardent advocate for integrating these technologies, Thomas Friedman (2013) argues that the massive online format represents the next evolution in higher education. As Friedman notes, this will have decidedly positive effect by improving "education outcomes in measurable ways at lower costs." Prospective college students or their parents, at least those who are savvy consumers, will question the value of tuition when the equivalent information can be obtained from an online course that is essentially free.[1] In supporting this view, Friedman (2013) points out that Michael Sandel, a distinguished political philosopher, will soon offer his highly regarded course on justice through a joint MIT-Harvard online delivery system. His lectures have already received more than 20 million views through Chinese websites alone. Already, one institution, San Jose State University in California, recently announced plans to offer "for-credit courses" using this technology (Markoff 2013a).

For advocates like Friedman, the massive online format is the future, bright and shiny. Viewed through the framework of counterrevolution, it seems to be yet another recapitulation of the sullied past. The technology is not the problem. Instead, it is the use made of that technology that is in contention here. Rather than serve the critical gestures of an authentic future, the MOOC represents another acquiescence to the power structures of the past. The massive online format was not developed altruistically, but as "a clear business model" for the aim of profiting private firms and funding universities. (Markoff 2012). As in the past, the technology is deployed to further weaken the status of the worker. Friedman appears somewhat oblivious (or indifferent) to this when he notes:

> We demand that plumbers and kindergarten teachers be certified to do what they do, but there is no requirement that college professors know how to teach. No more. The world of MOOCs is creating a competition that will force every professor to improve his or her pedagogy or face an online competitor. (Friedman 2013)

We have seen this future before. Hardly a harbinger of something new, this is the all-too familiar pattern of history, with the tendrils of industrial capitalism becoming further insinuated into the university. The traditional forms of labor cannot withstand the onslaught of cheaper and faster means of production. Like so much capital, masses of students will be accumulated by fewer and fewer instructors desperate to maintain their positions. Despite the success that Sandel, and others, have had Friedman (2013) acknowledges that some instructors will have global followings while others will not. This seems bound to expand the ongoing trend in which an increasing share of teaching is handled by shamefully low-compensated adjuncts and graduate students. The oversupply of individuals with doctoral degrees coupled with the artificial scarcity of regular, full-time faculty status positions has created a massive labor reserve. Neophyte academics cling to these poorly paid, overworked adjunct jobs, which often carry no health or retirement benefits, in order to maintain some fleeting toehold in academia, a denigrating compromise to justify the expense, labor, and time spent earning an advanced degree. June and Newman (2013) report that the average compensation for a three-credit course taught by an adjunct is just under $3,000. Of course, this means that someone in that position would have to teach ten courses per year to make just $30,000 before taxes. By comparison, an assistant professor at a public, doctorate-granting institution, earns on average $73,000 for teaching four courses per year (Jaschik 2013). However, not all adjuncts are so poorly compensated. Senator Marco Rubio, Republican from the state of Florida, was reportedly paid $24,000 to co-teach four classes per year at Florida International University, effectively double the regular adjunct rate (Clark 2011). Even more generously, retired Army General David Petraeus was offered $200,000 to teach one course at the City University of New York (Peralta 2013). After the website Gawker.com compared that figure to the $25,000 an adjunct at CUNY could normally expect to receive for working multiple courses, Petraeus agreed to work for $1, placing him firmly into the category of regular adjunct degradation.

Meanwhile, the decline of the human academic drags forward. EdX, a nonprofit company "founded by Harvard and the Massachusetts Institute of Technology" unveiled new software that effectively "uses artificial intelligence to grade student essays" (Markoff 2013b). With this development, it becomes conceivable for a course enrolling thousands of students to be hosted by a single instructor, or even the recording of an instructor. While Markoff suggests this technology will offer professors "a break," he seems naïve or indifferent to the likelihood that such a break will probably arrive in the form of early retirement or unemployment due to obsolescence. The need for human beings in education can be greatly reduced, as it has in practically every other industry, since the process of instruction can be largely automated. In effect, combining these two technologies—massive online courses and essay grading software—together allows for the reduction of human labor in education to the smallest fraction possible. Indeed, since the MOOC is recorded, the human element can be eliminated from education altogether. Some, such as Jacobs (2013) may doubt that this technology will represent the end of higher education in its present form, but one can just as easily imagine the fully online university eventually giving way to the fully *automated university*. It may seem like a product of science fiction or paranoia, but so were the robots that replaced assembly-line workers at Ford and General Motors who might have imagined their long-term employment prospects secure. Those academics opposing this trend will be, as Friedman already seems to imply, portrayed as archaic or antiquarian, afraid of progress, and embarrassing anachronisms. So was the traditional workman before the factory consumed his way of life and turned him into "the most wretched of commodities" (Marx 1998, p. 69). Quality is replaced by quantity and overwhelmed by concerns for the lowest possible cost to the university. There seems little in the way of a genuine future in a program designed to promote the mass society and the further subordination of life to a stultifying use of technology. Indeed, the outcome of such efforts seems to guarantee that there will be no future.

A cautious reader might question the use of the term 'future' here. It seems reasonable to propose at least two ways of articulating this concept. In one sense, the future is merely that expanse of time unfolding after the present. Under this view, the future cannot be prevented, provided that time itself continues on.[2] But that is not really the use of the term as I employ it here. Rather, the future ought to be understood as a paradig matically political shift (to borrow from Thomas Kuhn's lexicon), an as-yet-unseen fundamentally different social situation. Fredric Jameson speaks clearly to how visions of the future rarely exceed the parameters of the past and present. As he notes, utopian depictions of "streamlined cities" were little more than amplifications of the industrial settings in which they were conceived. Jameson (2005, 286) then points out, "That particular Utopian future has in other words turned out to have been merely the future of one moment of what is now our own past." The world of capitalism was quite literally unimaginable to the medieval mind. This conceptualization of the term "future"—a meaningful future as opposed to the inexorable and dreary procession of inevitability—refers to the chance for a different vision, a fundamental alternative to the present order. As Jameson again notes:

> The fundamental dynamic of any Utopian politics (or of any political Utopianism) will therefore always lie in the dialectic of Identity and Difference, to the degree to which such a politics aims at imagining, and sometimes even at realizing, a system radically different from this one. (Jameson 2005, p. xii)

No one would make the mistake of confusing the present with a utopia, or at least no one should. Marcuse (1970b, p. 63) explains that utopia "refers to projects for social change that are considered impossible." Utopian projects cannot be installed in the present, and in this sense the two translations of the word from ancient Greek—"good place" and "no place"—are concurrently true. The future remains, therefore, the terrain of utopian promise.

It is the singular aim of the combined counterrevolutionary projects to prevent a genuine future and merely extend past and present structures of domination through a variety of methods and tactics. Counterrevolution opposes a real future. It is the historical prevention of the utopian.[3] The science fiction film *The Terminator* (1984) expresses this essential aim of counterrevolution. A machine intelligence named Skynet, waging war with humanity in a nuclear decimated future, sends a cybernetic assassin back in time in order to destroy John Connor, the human leader, by killing his mother before he can even be conceived. Eliminating Connor in the year 2026 makes no difference. While his assassination might serve a symbolic value, he has already organized the human resistance, which has all but won. Connor's mother, Sarah, is not merely the target of the film's eponymous assassin because her death prevents John's life, but because she *trained* him and "taught her son to fight, organize, and prepare from when he was a kid." Sarah Connor is the target more so than her son because she represents the political education necessary for developing a revolutionary consciousness. The central conflict of *The Terminator* is not waged to alter the year 1984, nor is it fought in 2026, the setting of its narrative present. Rather, the mechanical assassin works to prevent revolutionary consciousness from coming into being in order to prohibit the composition of an entirely new future.

Thus far, I have examined different aspects of the counterrevolution and how it is manifested in the politics of reason. While Marcuse offers serious observations on the subject, the concept of counterrevolution largely remains adrift from the remainder of his work. That is, Marcuse himself never really situated his commentary on this theme within the larger scheme of his thinking. In this chapter, I want to demonstrate that, far from being a detached appendix hastily conjured toward the end of his career, counterrevolution actually unifies several important aspects of Marcuse's writing and brings his works into a more thoroughgoing conversation with other writers of the utopian genre, especially the Marxism of Fredric Jameson. This demonstration, however, goes beyond a purely exegetical exercise. It provides a vantage from which to observe exactly how counterrevolution functions in opposition to utopianism.

Counterrevolution establishes a repressive conduit between the one-dimensional subject and the political unconscious, but it does so, not for the present as the politics of that framework have already been constituted, but for a future that it must prevent. In the next section, I will elucidate the meanings of what Marcuse termed "surplus-repression" and the "one-dimensional" subject. At the same time, I will start to draw a link to Frederic Jameson's views on the "political unconscious." Following that, I will argue that the product of counterrevolution is a repressive conduit linking these concepts together. Finally, I argue that while this conduit transfers the horizons of imagination away from the one-dimensional subject, it simultaneously conveys surplus-repression back to the one-dimensional subject in the form of a moral prohibition against utopianism. Put differently, the common aim of all counterrevolutionary tactics in the politics of reason is to limit the imagination of the subject, increase the volume of the political unconscious, and preserve utopianism as the paramount *political obscenity*.

A PLAGUE OF NARROWED HORIZONS

Marcuse's most unique and valuable contribution to critical theory is arguably his politicization of Freudian thought. Pushing it beyond sterile, clinical parameters, Marcuse passes psychoanalysis through a Marxist framework and situates it within the context of historical materialism. Rather than merely leave Freud's concepts as suspiciously trans-historical, Marcuse insists that we historicize them. Of course, for Marx and Engels, history is the unfolding of class struggle, but the means by which that narrative progresses is thoroughly constrained. "Men make their own history," Marx writes (1963, p. 15), "but they do not make it just as they please." History contours the present like a "nightmare on the brain of the living." The options of the present are largely permutations of historical events. Those events, the options and choices of a given moment, are supplied by a material base. To briefly recapitulate an earlier point, the possibilities of the present are structured by the available technological and material resources.[4] Thus, the material base changes the "superstructure," the ideational forces within a historical moment such as religion, politics, ideology, divisions of labor, and so forth. When the base undergoes a sufficiently radical development (turning, for example, from the exploitation of animals to steam engines), then a reorganization of the superstructure will follow. A radical change in the base will lead to a massive reordering of the superstructure, a revolutionary change. Following this shift, base and superstructure become fundamentally different from the previous "mode of production." Each mode of production contains its own unique material forces and, therefore, its own unique class conflicts. As technology develops, history shapes and reshapes the character of society.

In any form of capitalism, the owners of the means of production demand that the worker labors to create a certain amount of value, but only pays that worker for a negligible fraction of what is generated. The excess, which the owner retains, is what Marx called "surplus value." It is derived from proletarian labor for which the capitalist essentially pays nothing. While the worker creates value for an entire day, the owner purchases only part of that value As Marx explains:

> Half the working day costs capital *nothing*; it thus obtains a value for which it has given no equivalent. And the multiplication of values can take place only if a value in excess of the equivalent has been obtained, hence *created*. Surplus value in general is value in excess of the equivalent. (Marx 1993, p. 324)

Thus, if a worker labors for the duration of an eight-hour shift, he or she might generate $100 in value for the firm, but will only be paid a fraction of that value and, generally speaking, that fraction will be the slimmest possible.[5] The worker creates that amount within the first part of the day, but most continue working in order to create the surplus-value for someone else. Marx (1976, p. 712) explains that the worker is only paid *after* he or she has "realized both the value of his labor-power and a certain quantity of surplus-value in the shape of commodities."

Using surplus-value as his point of departure, Marcuse applies the tenets of historical materialism to Freudian psychoanalysis starting from the "pleasure principle." This most essential of Freud's observations stipulates that, in the absence of any other constraints, human beings would seek out pleasure and avoid pain (Freud 1961, p. 25). Humans desire not merely the avoidance of pain and unpleasantness, but an intensification of pleasure as well (Freud 1966, p. 356). But as Marcuse (1955, p. 16) reminds us, *Ananke* or scarcity, rudely intervenes and disrupts the quest for uninterrupted pleasure. Devoting all of one's time to pleasurable pursuits would be tantamount to death by exhaustion or starvation. In order to obtain some pleasure, self-preservation is necessary. The individual forgoes the desire for constant pleasure in order to avoid death and procure the possibility of punctuated pleasure. Hence, the reality principle subdues the pleasure principle, though without extinguishing it entirely.

According to Freudian thought, tools that make survival easier become desirable insofar as they are also effectively instruments of pleasure. Insofar as they offer greater efficiency, these tools make procuring the objects of survival somewhat easier, leaving more time available for pleasurable pursuits. Freud (1961, p. 73) reasoned that one such invention was civilization itself. Cooperation equates to more effective labor, as the efforts of the many are better able to provide for survival than the individual. However, Marcuse points out that while civilization should permit more time for the pursuit of pleasure, it actually accomplishes just the opposite. Despite forming for the advantages of mutual cooperation, the distribution of labor does not occur according to any principle of equality. Most inhabitants of civilization toil well beyond what is necessary so that a few might profit. The great preponderance of human beings work to exhaustion so that the privileged can maintain far more leisure time and wealth than they could ever expend. Thus, for the great majority of human beings, the exploitative nature of civilization imposes[5] far more restrictions on the pursuit of pleasure than is actually necessary for survival, or, as Marcuse calls it, "surplus-repression." In the same manner as the capitalist extracts surplus-value from the laborer, the oppressed class is made to endure more labor than the demands of *ananke* would otherwise require. As they work beyond what is necessary, the capitalist is able to work less. It is the capitalist who recovers the time lost by the worker, who endures "additional controls over and above those indispensable for civilized human association" (Marcuse 1955, p. 37). Indeed, for Marcuse (1972b, p. 3), the degree of production achieved by capitalism would suggest that scarcity has long been overwhelmed. Where *Ananke* exists now, it is artificially induced (as a weapon of war, or a strategy of profit).

Repression is a cost of civilization. In order to better provide for our individual survival, cooperation demands eschewing the unrestricted pursuit of pleasure. Still, the debt of survival is not paid equally among all the members of civilization. Surplus-repression is not the accidental result of civilization. It is a means to domination, and its preservation is central to maintaining hierarchies of power (Marcuse 1955, p. 35). In that sense, surplus-repression refers to the unnecessary, additional repression some fraction of civilization imposes on the individual. Left to nothing but the pleasure principle, the individual is free to pursue as much pleasure in as many ways as he or she desires. In civilization, additional kinds of pleasure become prohibited. One is no longer free to use as much time as he or she can in obtaining pleasure, and some pleasures are categorically forbidden. In a system predicated on inequality much of our time is spent working, preparing for work, going to work, leaving work, and then endlessly repeating that cycle. A modicum of time remains for pursuing pleasure, but even this so-called free time is not exactly free. There are taboos and restrictions to consider. For countless others who may have to work multiple jobs, or those who have savagely limitless workdays, there may be no free time whatsoever.

The success of surplus-repression is owed largely to the production of an acquiescent subject, Marcuse's one-dimensional man. Industrial society forecloses as many alternatives as possible, limiting the imagination to think beyond the given system. Rather than, as it is commonly given, a realm of freedom, modern society is essentially totalitarian, suppressing "independence of thought, autonomy, and the right to political opposition" (Marcuse 1964, p. 1). Anticipating our prejudices, Marcuse assures us that totalitarianism is not necessarily identical with a police state. It proceeds instead "through the manipulation of needs," persuading the masses to eagerly comply and identify the wares of the system as indispensible (ibid., p. 3). The values of the Establishment permeate every aspect of society, politics, and culture, or, as Marcuse states:

> The power over man which this society has acquired is daily absolved by its efficacy and productiveness. If it assimilates everything it touches, if it absorbs the opposition, if it plays with the contradiction, it demonstrates its cultural superiority. (ibid., pp. 84–85)

The effect of this kind of social organization is the steady diminishing of intellect and free thought. Indeed, the individual is confined to an ever-smaller universe of alternatives in action and thought that are supplied beneath a façade of freedom. "Liberty," Marcuse (1964, p. 7) explains, "can be made into a powerful instrument of domination." One is free to choose from a vast array of products and services within the system, but the system itself is never subject to choosing. Again, Marcuse (1964, p. 7) states, "Free election of masters does not abolish the masters or the slaves." The individual that remains is effectively "one-dimensional," robbed of the ability to exhibit any sort of utopian gestures. Instead of an individual capable of critically assessing his or her world, capitalism "has stifled the emergence of such a consciousness and imagination" (Marcuse 1969, p. 15). As domination permeates, the individual becomes less able to think beyond the horizons established by the system. The permissible realities imposed by capitalism constrain the limits of thought and action (Marcuse 1964, p. 12). In effect, the one-dimensional society begets subjects that can neither think nor act beyond the narrow limits it provides. Class society has "shaped the sensibility and the reason of man" just as it has "shaped the freedom of the imagination" (Marcuse 1969, p. 29). Alternatives to capitalism are dismissed as mere utopianism in the most pejorative, unrealistic sense. Those alternatives become, in a very real way, unimaginable. It would seem, therefore, that the first step toward installing surplus-repression and extracting surplus-value is the totalitarian spread of capitalist culture, a plague of narrowed horizons.

THE REPRESSIVE CONDUIT

If the one-dimensional subject is generated by a narrowing of the imaginative horizons, then we ought to regard Fredric Jameson's "political unconscious" as the repository for that purloined mental content. It is a forbidden library, a space created by capitalist suppression cataloging alternative political possibilities. The political unconscious is the terrain of the depoliticized, the repository of lost critical content. Late capitalism conceals the political and social dimensions inherent to literature and other narrative forms. In this regard, capitalism "maims our existence as individual subjects and paralyzes our thinking about time and change just as surely as it alienates us from our speech itself" (Jameson 1981, p. 20). This disfigurement is an effect of an expression of power in which the political is repackaged as apolitical.

Whereas Jameson (1981, p. 20) asserts the imperative of recognizing "that there is nothing that is not social and historical—indeed, that everything is 'in the last analysis' political," capitalism divests literature, art, and other kinds of discourse of their political content, leaving only a kind of bankrupt spectacle. In this manner, the work of art—a painting or science fiction film—can be invalidated, precluded from serious commentary or bearing the signs of politics; it is merely "art" in the most condescending sense possible. Seidman (1996, 713n1) points out that the labeling of some object as art further silences and marginalizes other forms which, in addition to being depoliticized, are prohibited from even bearing artistic value. Of course the categorization of art or literature as apolitical is itself a profoundly political gesture, an act that effectively conceals itself within the political unconscious along with the other artifacts stowed in that lost space. As Jameson explains:

> Unfortunately, no society has ever been quite so mystified in quite so many ways as our own, saturated as it is with messages and information, the very vehicles of mystification (language, as Talleyrand put it, having been given us in order to conceal our thoughts). If everything were transparent, then no ideology would be possible, and no domination either: evidently that is not our case. (Jameson 1981, p. 61)

Hence, the political unconscious is a repository; a space in which a vast field of suppressed political content has been concealed by the mystifying, depoliticizing efforts of late capitalism. Jameson (2005, p. xiii) alerts us to this fundamental problem in which "our imaginations are hostages to our own mode of production (and perhaps to whatever remnants of past ones it has preserved)." The ability to even think beyond capitalism is badly deformed, if not altogether repressed. Alternative possibilities are instantly dismissed as fanciful, pejoratively Utopian, and dangerous; if such thoughts can even be entertained, they are assigned the neutered label of mere entertainment.

It would be an oversight, perhaps dangerously so, to presume that surplus-repression, the one-dimensional man, or the political unconscious are static or somehow fixed. I suggest here that the tactics of the counterrevolution serve as a bridge linking the space of the political unconscious and the one-dimensional subject of late capitalism. The neutralization of revolutionary consciousness, alienation of reason, dissemination of consumer ideology, and draining of the aesthetic dimension within teaching all share the effect of constraining the intellect of the subject. In essence, the various tactics of the counterrevolution establish a repressive conduit, siphoning off the political imagination of an increasingly one-dimensional subject and transporting this excised consciousness into the space of the political unconscious.

At the site of the individual, counterrevolution succeeds by closing the space of reason, crippling the development of critical and intellectual faculties. The horizons of the individual are narrowed. In doing so, counterrevolutionary tactics expand the political unconscious, transferring more and more content into the realm of the apolitical. This forecloses the viability of alternatives and criticisms to the system. Hence, the aggrandizement of the political unconscious results in the pervasiveness of the one-dimensional subject and the generalized compliance to surplus-repression. Put differently, as the political unconscious grows, thanks to a successful counterrevolutionary effort, the political conscious shrinks, the universe of discourse shrinks, and the subject of late capitalism becomes increasingly conformist, unimaginative, politically meek, and one-dimensional. Surplus-repression then goes uncontested.

These observations might be objected on the basis that we inhabit what is essentially a less repressed environment when compared with earlier eras in American history. After all, Marcuse (1969, p. 9) notes that the display of the naked body, despite supposedly being obscene, is encouraged and "taboos on pre-marital and extra-marital intercourse are considerably relaxed." People are freer to talk about sex and sexuality. It appears with greater frequency in art and entertainment. And, indeed, laws allowing individuals of the same sex to marry are becoming increasingly common. The problem is that none of these supposed "freedoms" have transpired beyond a system of exploitation. Expanding on his earlier statement, Marcuse reminds us that the illusion of freedom is often promoted as another means of domination:

> Under the rule of the repressive whole, liberty can be made into a powerful instrument of domination. The range of choice open to the individual is not the decisive factor in determining the degree of human freedom, but *what* can be chosen and what *is* chosen by the individual. (Marcuse 1964, p. 7)

If people of the same sex have been permitted to marry, it is only after first being identified and categorized as a new consumer group—homosexual—and then directed toward a model of monogamous marriage that is already situated within the reach of profit and social utility.[6] While no one should be denied the dignity of a basic right, it is highly dubious as an act of freedom.[7] Likewise, the representation of sexuality in media, while certainly interesting to look at, cannot be mistaken for real freedom when it serves corporate interests and, more often than not, the further mystification of the masses. Here Marcuse (1978, p. 40) explains, "Both obscenity and pornography have long since been integrated. As commodities they too communicate the repressive whole." Repression is most effective when it is mistaken as an experience in freedom.

By neutralizing the possible sources of political education the Establishment is able to enlarge the political unconscious and preventatively ward off threats to the system. The tactics of counterrevolution act as a repressive conduit linking the one-dimensional subject with the political unconscious. It thereby serves to enhance both; by undermining reason it prevents the subject from accessing the political unconscious, thus maintaining its pernicious one-dimensional status. As an instrument of totalitarianism, the repressive conduit regulates the transfer of imagination, thereby reinforcing existing values and potentially adding new values. Counterrevolution defends the entrenchment of surplus-repression. Prohibited imagery is depoliticized and consigned to the political unconscious. Of course, this is not a matter of mind control and the idea of resistance, in various forms, persists (otherwise Mar-

cuse, Althusser, and Jameson would have had very little to write about).
However, that which cannot be submerged into the unconscious can be ridiculed and shamed within the realm of the politically conscious. What becomes part of the political unconscious, in such cases, is the possibility of
taking seriously the content of the categorically ridiculous. In that sense,
counterrevolutionary tactics cannot erase the ideas of resistance or revolution, but they can impose a value on those concepts and render them *obscene*.

THE POLITICAL OBSCENE

In Marcuse's view, obscenity is a prop, an instrument of power used to
suppress antithetical values. As he explains, "Obscenity is a moral concept in
the verbal arsenal of the Establishment, which abuses the term by applying it,
not to expressions of its own power but to those of another" (Marcuse 1969,
8). In other words, the Establishment applies the category of obscenity to
actions and ideas that it opposes. Conversely, those things that function in the
service of capitalism are unlikely to be portrayed as obscene, regardless of
how profane they might actually be. Accordingly, the one-dimensional subject, following the valuation of the Establishment, mistakes ideas and imagery of freedom for that of obscenity. As Marcuse notes:

> Obscene is not the picture of a naked woman who exposes her pubic hair but
> that of a fully clad general who exposes his medals rewarded in a war of
> aggression; obscene is not the ritual of the Hippies but the declaration of a high
> dignitary of the Church that war is necessary for peace. (ibid., p. 8)

Within the constellation of Establishment values, there is the clear delinea-
tion between the obscene and its antipode, the decent. Displays of nudity,
eroticism, and sexuality are associated with obscenity while displays of violence, bloodshed, and ostentatious wealth are acceptable.

Proceeding from the basis of historical materialism, obscenity assumes a
character that is peculiar to the mode of production; that which is obscene in
capitalism is not necessarily obscene during another historical epoch. Regardless of its peculiar historical content, the category of the obscene refers
to the depiction of indecency that ought to evoke a sensation of shame or
guilt (ibid., 8). That is, the sight or experience of obscenity should compel a
feeling of embarrassment for the normal individual. He explains that what
ought to be considered shameful—bloodshed and opulence in a world reek-
ing of poverty—are celebrated, while what ought to celebrated—sexuality
and eroticism—are considered shameful. For Marcuse, it is clear that any
normal individual ought to be embarrassed or ashamed at the sight of violence, not nudity. Yet, the entertainment of late capitalism suggests that
matters are precisely the opposite. Every viewer of television and film is

exposed to a virtually ceaseless torrent of bullets and blood. While still accessible, everyone knows that nudity and sexuality have reserved places that are supposedly hidden away from minors. They can, of course, still view these subjects but only while learning that they should not, that such matters have many more rules attached to them than a subject such as violence. For the most part, more people hide away their pornography than conceal bullet-ridden action films. There is shame in sexuality and very little attached to violence, which, generally speaking, is celebrated by the culture of the Establishment.

We are most familiar with the attachment of obscenity to the various categories of sexuality. However, if obscenity in general refers to imagery or ideas that ought to provoke a sense of shame or disgust, then it would seem applicable beyond the restricted realm of sexuality. Outside of erotic pursuits, there are those political images and ideas which, according to the Establishment, ought to provoke a sense of shame or disgust. While we are generally familiar with and *aware* of sexual obscenities, the political obscene operates on a more surreptitious level. If the obscene in general is that which ought to arouse a sensation of disgust, guilt, or shame, then erotic obscenities incite those feelings with regard to sexuality and desire. The political obscene refers to the domain of those ideas or imagery that provoke disgust, guilt, or shame arising from attempts to contemplate an organization of resources and power that is fundamentally alternative to the one provided by the Establishment.

Marcuse and Jameson point out in their respective works that individuals within late capitalism are systematically enfeebled from being able to imagine a world beyond capitalism. As Marcuse states:

> The power of corporate capitalism has stifled the emergence of such a consciousness and imagination; its mass media have adjusted the rational and emotional faculties to its market and its policies and steered them to defense of its dominion. (Marcuse 1969, p. 15)

Likewise Jameson (2005, p. 231) notes, "most of us are probably unconsciously convinced of these principles, and of the eternity of the system." However, we are not merely unable to break free of the one-dimensional horizons put before us, we are *ashamed* to even try. The repressive conduit created by counterrevolution does more than simply stifle the imagination. As part of the various counterrevolutionary efforts designed to limit the capability of thinking beyond the present system, the individual in capitalism is also expected to feel shame at even entertaining such a thought.

What, then, is politically obscene in late capitalism? The Establishment makes quite clear as to what ought to provoke shame and disgust—the depiction of uselessness. Decency is that which can be harnessed for profit or power, and it is worth recalling here the increasing demand for college education to service the economy. College education that becomes training in science and technology is promoted, while fields of study that have no clear vocational value are diminished. The obscene is nothing more than representations of that which the Establishment has yet to put in its service. Action that cannot be immediately appropriated for profit, or otherwise exploited, is labeled perverse. As Marcuse (1955, p. 49) notes, "The societal organization of the sex instinct taboos as *perversions* practically all its manifestations which do not serve or prepare for the procreative function." In terms of sexuality, those acts that do not have procreation as their ultimate aim are regarded as aberrations, and in the capitalist mode of production, a lack of utility signifies perversion. Obscenity is a representation of the perverse. Therefore, the depiction or representation of uselessness is *obscene* according to the demands of capitalist ideology. It stands to reason that the most obscene is also that which is most useless to the Establishment, and nothing is more useless, and therefore more obscene, than Utopia, that which gestures toward a fundamentally alternative future.

The tactics of counterrevolution are unified in creating a repressive conduit that narrows the horizons of the one-dimensional subject, expanding the repository of the political unconscious, stabilizing the burdens of surplus-repression, and preserving utopia and utopianism as the paramount political obscenity. That is, the various expressions of counterrevolution are designed to eliminate the faculties that might fulminate in revolutionary consciousness and maintain the myth of utopian impossibility and uselessness as unassailable. There is nothing more useless or bankrupt of utility than the impossible or deeply implausible. These are the prime indictments made against utopia and utopianism. Without ever saying what "it" actually is, utopia is most frequently dismissed under the aegis that "it would never work;" "it is impossible." Except to the exceedingly small minority who identify as utopians (such as Marcuse and Jameson), this is the common view of utopian thought. Even Friedrich Engels (1978, p. 687) participates in this derision, when he writes that Utopians would "evolve out of the human brain" solutions to material problems.

Of course, in describing utopianism as the paramount political obscenity, it might be objected that most people do not experience the same sense of revulsion that they would at the sight of child pornography, which is quite likely the paramount moral obscenity. Not all obscenities evoke the same intensity of feeling, but there seems to be little doubt that one *ought* to be ashamed for aspiring to such ridiculous thoughts as an alternative to capitalism. Thomas Sowell (2006, p. 104) mocks efforts for social justice as crusades betraying a delusional desire to "be on the side of the angels." Mark Lilla (2001, p. 214) warns that every man and woman harbors the "lure of Syracuse," a phrase invoking Plato's disastrous attempt to advise the tyrant

Dionysus II toward a more just politics. Syracuse is clearly a metaphor of a general desire to improve the conditions of our world. Restricted to conservative aims, this "urge" is acceptable. Clearly, a utopian gesture would be not merely inadvisable, but belonging to some alien fringe, or, as Lilla indicates:

> Today, in corners of left-leaning European bookshops, one can still find unwanted sets of Lenin's, Mao's, even Stalin's collected works, which were translated by propaganda bureaus in the Communist world and published by front organizations in the West. It may strike us as preposterous today that anyone would have felt the need to consult such works, or even to write them. (ibid., p. 207)

Preposterous indeed. And of course, one ought to be ashamed of dabbling in preposterousness.[8] There is nothing more obscene, more shameful, in the politics of the Establishment, than clinging to the idea of Utopia, than being a utopian. Marcuse (1970b, p. 63) tells us "utopia is a historical concept." If so, counterrevolution emerges in history as its nemesis. The triumph of counterrevolution is located in preserving the uselessness of utopianism. Criticism of the system is most often met with disdain and dismissal. Marcuse (1972b, p. 133) wryly noted, "Today it seems a crime merely to talk about change while one's society is transformed into an institution of violence, terminating in Asia the genocide which began with the liquidation of American Indians."

AGAINST THE COUNTERREVOLUTION

In March 2013, a communications instructor at Florida Atlantic University asked his students to take out a sheet of paper, and then told them to write the word "Jesus" on the sheet. He then suggested they place that paper on the floor and stomp on it. The discomfort they undoubtedly felt was meant to demonstrate the power of symbols. Predictably, one student complained and, even though the exercise was not mandatory, Governor Rick Scott demanded a thorough investigation (Jester 2013). The instructor since apologized for the exercise. Whether it was tactless or inadvisable is one matter. It seems unlikely that the instructor will lose his job, and he certainly should not. The investigation Scott wants will likely produce nothing of value, but the fact that he insinuated himself into an academic exercise points to a larger problem. Many more instructors will ask whether broaching a controversial topic is worthwhile, exercises of critical thinking will be weighed against the potential consequences for offending student-consumers, and the faculties of dissent will atrophy further.

In the era of counterrevolution, the politics of reason are manipulated to serve the ends of domination, narrowing the horizons of imagination through the production of a political obscene in which utopian gestures are firmly situated. Not quite part of the political unconscious, the utopian remains within the twilight of conscious thought where it is most often treated as an object of ridicule for its impracticality. The tactics of counterrevolution function for the maintenance of this strategic aim. The state exerts its power to shape the curriculum, diverting students and resources away from disciplines engaged in potentially critical thought and toward technical and commodifiable fields, aborting the intellect and neutralizing the development of a revolutionary consciousness before it can be conceived. Concurrently, the intellectual is represented in conservative discourse as an inhuman. Since the other-than-human is alien, then the medium of the intellectual, which is reason, must be the medium of an alien. Hence, reason can be more easily alienated. Meanwhile, the university has responded to counterrevolutionary influences by promoting the logic of consumerism. Rather than emphasize the production of workers, which can lead to a potentially subversive class consciousness, the focus has shifted to the production of consumers thereby reproducing the relations of consumption that leads only to an individuated, compliant consumer consciousness. And while the consumer is given at least the pretense of a wider universe of selections, the laborer is subject to the pressures of an increasingly narrowed range of options. Concurrently, the imposition of online teaching by state and administrative powers has become magnified, thus limiting the aesthetic possibilities available and the provocation of thinking that follows from diversity of form. The MOOC is the perverse synthesis of consumer consciousness and teaching in the age of electronic reproduction. Far from being a haven for egalitarian principles, it appears as one more artifact of the fascist aesthetic that Benjamin warns against. The purported virtue of the MOOC format is that it reaches a tremendous number of people, especially those who would be otherwise unable to obtain education. Adorno and Horkheimer, if not Benjamin before them, cautioned us to be wary of how domination is often clothed in the attractive fabrics of enlightenment. Despite their admonitions, the MOOC is yet another example of machinery enrapturing the mass society through spectacle and fascination. The participating professor substitutes for the figure of "glorious leader," becoming a comparatively minor object of authoritarian fascination.

The focus of this project has been to examine the tactics of counterrevolution as they pertained to "the school," broadly understood. In that sense, this has been an analysis of how counterrevolutionary efforts have successfully contested the politics of reason. The question might reasonably turn to consider whether or not counterrevolution in the politics of reason is exerted beyond the confines of schools and universities. I think the answer is resoundingly affirmative. There have been numerous efforts in recent years to turn back workers' rights, disenfranchise the poor from their political rights and sources of welfare, and concurrent efforts to saturate the individual with every product imaginable as a means to further install the false needs of the system. No one can do without a computer, a "smart" phone, and a host of other gadgets. Likewise, remedies for the financial crises created by the wealthy have largely come at the expense of the poor and poorer nations. Austerity measures do not seem borne equally. Indeed, it is almost difficult to ignore the various signs of counterrevolution. Still, some battlefields yield more identifiable casualties, and, beyond the politics of reason, the results can be fatal. Nevertheless, I have chosen to examine counterrevolution in the school because it is ideology and the struggle waged in the mind that makes the summary executions, massacres, and Disappeared possible in the first place.

Marx (1963, p. 15) observed that the past weighs like a nightmare on the brains of the living. Perhaps this is true of the Marxist trying to throw off what he calls the "muck of the ages" (Marx and Engels 1998, p. 60). For the Establishment, for the agents of counterrevolution, it seems more likely that the future, or some alternative iteration of it, is the terrifying dark horse. Marcuse draws our attention toward the unfolding of counterrevolution as a symptom of this fear. Accordingly, we ought to consider the derisions and summary dismissals that tend to arise in trying to imagine a future beyond capitalism. The refusals to even broach such possibilities occur reflexively, often without even realizing it. In essence, we are mostly unaware that shame is attached to political concepts. This is the repressive conduit at its most effective.

It is customary, at this point, to offer suggestions for confronting the tactics of counterrevolution. This is when the divide between the humanist and structuralist divisions within Marxism become most apparent. Resistance, as a practice, is always the most vexing question. The contributions of structuralist Marxism, as represented by Althusser, seem to teach that there is very little we can do, that any dissent we can postulate may be just another commodity of the system prepackaged as dissent. Yet, the humanist Marxism of Marcuse teaches us that we must do *something*. Obstacles, such as the exertion of state power on behalf of the Establishment, seem numerous and daunting. If Marcuse is correct, then perhaps the most serious of these impediments is located in our own already-narrowed imagination. That is, the efficacy of any solution that might be proposed has to be seriously doubted, as it may be nothing more than the product of a thoroughly repressed, one-dimensional imagination. The fruit of our minds may unwittingly provide sustenance to the machinations of the Establishment (and here Althusser's fatalism seems most plausible). Indeed, the momentum continues to drift in the wrong direction. Thomas Friedman is by no means alone in asserting that massive online courses are the wave of the future. If he were isolated in such sentiments, Professor Sandel's lectures would not have been accessed over twenty million times. Politicians from across the spectrum would not appear so united in promoting the study of STEM disciplines, and eager to obstruct accessibility to those disciplines promoting critical thought.

Marcuse dealt directly with the hope, and frustrating disappointments, for revolutionary change in a social sensibility labeled "the Great Refusal." Put simply, the Great Refusal, he (1955, p. 149) explains, "is the protest against unnecessary repression, the struggle for the ultimate form of freedom." Just as capitalism represents a totalizing and totalitarian system, the Great Refusal represents a totalizing revulsion against capitalism in all of its political, social, cultural, and economic manifestations. Thus Marcuse, observes that the Refusal can be identified with guerrilla wars in opposition to imperialism, as well as "student opposition" and the deployment of obscenities and other countercultural practices (Marcuse 1969, pp. viii and 8). In effect, the Great Refusal denotes a necessary step toward establishing the freedom of an unrepressed society. As Marcuse writes:

> Meanwhile there are the enslaved human beings who must accomplish their own liberation. To develop their conscience and consciousness, to make them aware of what is going on, to prepare the precarious ground for the future alternatives—this is our task: "our" not only as Marxists but as intellectual, and that means all those who are still free and able to think by themselves and against indoctrination, communist as well as anticommunist." (Marcuse 1965, p. 109)

Yet, even as the Great Refusal started to gain momentum, it was already becoming undermined from within by an array of counterrevolutionary forces. The political consciousness and resistances of the 1960s steadily capitulated and gave way to the consumerism, indifference, and reactionary attitudes of the 1980s. Just at the moment when it seemed possible for the Establishment to crumble, the hippies dispersed, the Black Panthers were disrupted, and the revolutions of China, Cuba, and Vietnam became suspiciously un-revolutionary. Despite the many gains toward advancing progressive social change, as Bronner (2011, p. 90) puts it, "The marginal groups were perhaps never quite that marginal." The working and middle classes largely sold out, and the disaffected traded in the counterculture of the 1960s for BMWs and corporate careers of the 1980s.[9] The Great Refusal, refusing only itself, became the Great Capitulation.

The Great Refusal failed because of the ongoing counterrevolution, which continues to function in order to thwart future irruptions of dissent. That is, the present counterrevolution is designed precisely to render futile the imagination of a remedy for its effects. Are there plausible lines of resistance? In classical Marxism, revolution does not transpire until the proletariat seizes the means of production. Only by controlling the factories and resources can there be fundamental change. Of course, in order to seize the means of production, the proletariat must adopt a revolutionary consciousness. Any possible revolution hinges on that crucial necessity, and it is for that reason that the school is a largely uncontested instrument of counterrevolution. All I can suggest are possible avenues of contestation, preludes or preliminaries. If taken as keys to unlocking revolution, they will be most unsatisfactory, but I believe they can address the more limited aim of contesting counterrevolution.

If struggle over the politics of reason is most acutely located in the space of the school, then it falls upon those of us most directly engaged in that location to consider how we are uniquely suited to contest this matter. The aim of counterrevolution turns on two subjects: the student and the intellectual. Control of the former through acquiescence of the latter remains the real goal of counterrevolutionary power. As teachers, we are limited, as Althusser reminds us, precisely inasmuch as we are appendages of the Ideological State Apparatus. Educators, whether in public or private schools, lower or higher education, are always employees. In that regard, before we are teachers, we must embrace our role as intellectuals.

Frederic Jameson (2005, 171n3) explains that anti-intellectualism is a central component of "anti-Utopianism." That is, the efforts to weaken Utopian projects employ "a certain popular philistinism" that relies on the "hatred of intellectuals" (ibid., p. 190). For these reasons, rather than deflect criticism of the intellectual by way of another limp denial, we ought to embrace the dangerousness of our profession and be unashamed to perform the work of demystification, political education, and decide which is preferable: adopting the potentially arrogant language of critical theory with its elitist notions of false and true consciousness, or the politically aimless content of post-structuralism that often replaces anything resembling genuine political concerns with an unnecessarily inaccessible argot. I accept the accusation that critical theory is fraught with elitism, but post-structuralism has lapsed into an excuse to do nothing. As Marcuse (1969, 6) indicates, resistance may turn on the "radical transvaluation of values." Rather than deny our elitism, arrogance, and dangerousness, we ought to embrace those accusations as virtues and put them to work toward political education.

The point is best captured in one of Marcuse's more controversial essays, entitled "Repressive Tolerance." In considering the exercise of speech in the West, Marcuse (1970a, p. 88) states that there should be no tolerance for the expression of harmful ideas, or as, he writes, our principles "cannot protect false words and wrong deeds which demonstrate that they counteract the possibilities of liberation." This statement was the source of considerable controversy, with claims that Marcuse undermined the cause of freedom by favoring censorship and was guilty of "double standards" (Kors and Silverglate 1998, p. 69). However, such accusations vastly distort his position. After all, Marcuse makes no gesture in favor of curtailing speech through the exercise of state power (*as if such an idea was even possible for a thinker who understood the state to be nothing more than an executor of the ruling class*). Rather, Sowell, Lilla, Johnson and others are legally entitled to say and write whatever they will. That does not mean that their ideas have to be tolerated. Their anti-intellectual invective and vitriol ought not go unchallenged, contested, and repudiated. Intellectuals on the left should not be cowed from action, especially by the possibility of being labeled elitist or arrogant. Marcuse recognized the centrality of teachers and intellectuals, critics and criticism, in confronting the suppression of revolutionary consciousness. He writes:

> It is the task and duty of the intellectual to recall and preserve historical possibilities which seem to have become utopian possibilities—that it is his task to break the concreteness of oppression in order to open the mental space in which this society can be recognized as what it is and does. (Marcuse 1970, p. 81)

Educators should not be intimidated into censoring themselves for fear that they may end up on a list of leftists. Those who are willing ought to do the work of political education. [10] We can be effective at this end, in our classrooms, every day. As Jameson concurs:

> Hence, the ludicrous, silly, and preposterous ideas, the outlandish proposals to escape from a system of domination and exploitation have to be recovered. It is the role of the intellectual to resist the expansion of the political unconscious. Ultimately, the task we are left with is trying to recover the political content of "the cultural past (and present) which we didn't see before (or didn't want to see before)." (Jameson 2007, p. 42)

Consensus and agreement are scarce resources, but we have an obligation to recognize our potential to resist exploitative schemes on the part of politicians, administrators, and even of our own devising, or we can become the implements of counterrevolutionary interpellation, the tools of counterrevolution. As educators, whether in universities, community colleges, or primary and secondary schools, we ought to oppose the denigration of social sciences, arts, and humanities and the STEM-oriented valuation of education as an exercise in commercially utilizable vocational training. We ought to resist the imposition of an electronic aesthetic on education and Thomas Friedman's regurgitation of the industrial methods of production by way of massive courses. However, in thinking dialectically, we also ought to recognize the potential of this technology in being used toward *revolutionary* rather than counterrevolutionary ends. In this era of counterrevolution, it seems more likely than not that a massive online course will be harnessed toward the ends of mystification, but it also bears the potential for use in the raising of consciousness in a heretofore unprecedented way. As Marx alerts us and

Marcuse reminds us, technology can be used for nefarious as well as emancipative ends.

Students also have an important role to play in struggling over the politics of reason. In fact, students, precisely because they are not employees or appendages of the state apparatus, bear far more power than they think. As the consumers of the university product, students are uniquely situated to oppose, en masse, the redirection toward a technical curriculum, the degradation of standards, overcrowding of classrooms, consumerist orientation, and persistent expansion of online teaching. At a large institution, even a fraction of the overall student body, peacefully and publicly performing the acts of refusal at the centers of administrative power would represent a massive voice of discontent. As consumers, it is the students who must reject the product they are being sold, a product the value of which is falsely advertised and the quality of which continues declining toward unacceptable standards. Such acts, modeled on the organic outbursts of the Occupy movement, but more clearly focused on manageable goals, might carry the promise of the Great Refusal on a more modest scale. They could at least secure the conditions for the reproduction of the relations of dissent.

Even if these suggestions are deemed unacceptable, it remains crucial that we consider possible lines of resistance, if for no other reason than to exercise the atrophied imagination. It is necessary, however, that we recognize the character and context of resistance. Nothing I propose here exceeds the parameters of capitalism. Marx has already taught us that the sole condition for authentic revolution is the seizure of the means of production. Anything short of that is unrevolutionary. Counterrevolution serves to obstruct the development of a revolutionary consciousness. My purpose is not to supply a path to revolution, which is completely beyond my purview and imagination, but the comparatively modest aim of inaugurating the basis for restoring the nemesis of counterrevolution, which is refusal.

Capitalism exerts itself on a global scale and represents the "ultimate horizon," as Jameson (2006, p. 8) describes it. Institutions will continue to reflect the objectives of the prevailing power, which is ultimately an expression of who or what owns the means of production. Circumventing the tactics of counterrevolution is simply unfeasible. Protesting students and agitating intellectuals, whether in front of administrative centers or in the streets of Paris, London, and Montreal, are not going to unleash a global revolution, but they can struggle for the consciousness of the future. Of course, if students are going to rally in opposition to the deteriorating conditions of education, they must first have the necessary consciousness to recognize that the conditions have deteriorated. And that raises the prior demand for effective political education under counterrevolutionary conditions that make all such resistance increasingly difficult and unlikely. Still, difficulty is not the same as impossibility and some gestures of refusal remain. The first step is to continue what Marcuse started by pointing to the signs of counterrevolution.

Just as the varied tactics of counterrevolution are unified by the repressing the faculties of dissent, student and educator ought to share the common commitments of celebrating reason and praising the intellectual (by which I mean both the theme of that which is intellectual and the intellectual as category of person). Should that fail, I am reminded here of the yarn about Diogenes the Cynic. When asked by visitors to Athens the whereabouts of the popular politician Demosthenes, Diogenes extended his middle finger and said, "This is the great demagogue of the Athenian people" (Diogenes Laertius 1901, p. 229). Such a gesture by intellectuals and their students against the abuses of the Establishment and its agents seems fitting. Yet, if it appears to be nothing more than a sophomoric, unintelligent expression of frustration, then perhaps that is because obscenity is all that remains to the one-dimensional mind in this age of counterrevolution.

NOTES

1. They are free, notwithstanding the cost of a computer and viable Internet connection, which admittedly are almost essential (and dubious) prerequisites for any college experience in this era.

2. I will leave that question to the physicists.

3. One might argue that it also resists the dystopian. However, I would argue that term, dystopia, is easily applicable for the present world. As Marcuse (1970b, 64) notes, "All the material forces which could be put to work for the realization of a free society are at hand." We possess the technological and material capabilities to overwhelm scarcity and poverty. Those capabilities, however, are put to use for decidedly irrational and destructive ends. How else could such a perversion of potential be described than as dystopian?

4. Choosing to land on the moon is not an available option during the era of the steam engine, for example.

5. This would constitute a relatively generous allotment on the part of the capitalist.

6. A number of the conservative commentators to openly support same-sex marriage have done so on the basis that it promotes "the family unit" (Portman 2013) or because "it would be a civilizing force for gay people too" (Carlson 2007).

7. Herein lies the important distinction and tension between Marx's concept of political emancipation (greater freedoms within the given system) and universal human emancipation (freedom from the system itself). For Marx, it is clearly the latter which is more desirable, but the more acts of emancipation the Establishment can be seen dispensing the better able it is to conceal the oppressive nature of its system.

8. I would identify neither Mao nor Stalin with desirable visions of the future. Lilla's act of association between these architects of mass murder and Lenin is crude, if not altogether misleading. If nothing else, they represent alternatives—leftist bogeymen—in the politics of those like Lilla and Sowell. For those reasons only, they have some value.

9. Worst of all, Jefferson Airplane turned into Jefferson Starship.

10. In that sense, I vehemently oppose the position taken by Stanley Fish (2008) in which politics have no bearing in the classroom. While Fish might argue that we have no business indoctrinating students, he ignores, or conceals, the underlying fact that this opposition to indoctrination is itself another kind of indoctrination. Indeed, it is liberal indoctrination masquerading as apolitical education. For the critical theorist, no such thing as value-free education exists.

Works Cited

Ahmari, Sohrab. "How Free Speech Died on Campus." In the *Wall Street Journal.* November 16, 2012.

Allen, Greg. "Gov. Scott, Ex-CEO, Aims to Run Fla. Like a Business." On National Public Radio. January 6, 2011. www.npr.org/2011/01/06/132684525/rick-scott-floridas-outsider-is-now-in-office

Allen, I. Elaine, and Jeff Seaman. "Going the Distance: Online Education in the United States, 2011." *Babson Survey Research Group.* November 2011.

Althusser, Louis. 1990a. "Philosophy and the Spontaneous Philosophy of the Scientists." In *Philosophy and the Spontaneous Philosophy of the Scientists.* Ed. Gregory Elliott. London: Verso.

Althusser, Louis. 1990b. "The Transformation of Philosophy." In *Philosophy and the Spontaneous Philosophy of the Scientists.* Ed. Gregory Elliott. London: Verso.

Althusser, Louis. 1996. *For Marx.* Trans. Ben Brewster. New York: Verso.

Althusser, Louis. 2001a. "Philosophy as a Revolutionary Weapon." In *Lenin and Philosophy and Other Essays.* Ed. Frederic Jameson. New York: Monthly Review Press.

Althusser, Louis. 2001b. "Ideology and Ideological State Apparatuses." In *Lenin and Philosophy and Other Essays.* Ed. Frederic Jameson. New York: Monthly Review Press.

Althusser, Louis. 2001c. "Lenin and Philosophy." In *Lenin and Philosophy and Other Essays.* Ed. Frederic Jameson. New York: Monthly Review Press.

Althusser, Louis. 2001d. "Cremonini, Painter of the Abstract." In *Lenin and Philosophy and Other Essays.* Ed. Frederic Jameson. New York: Monthly Review Press.

Althusser, Louis. 2001e. "A Letter on Art in Reply to Andre Daspre." In *Lenin and Philosophy and Other Essays.* Ed. Frederic Jameson. New York: Monthly Review Press.

Anderson, Patrick. "Walker Education Plan Gets Mixed Reviews." In *LaCrosse Tribune.* January 20, 2012. www.lacrossetribune.com/news/local/walker-education-plan-gets-mixed-reviews/article_26b9f0de-431b-11e1-a5bb-001871e3ce6c.html

Anderson, Zac. "Rick Scott Wants to Shift University Funding Away from Some Degrees." In *Sarasota Herald-Tribune.* October 10, 2011. www.htpolitics.com/2011/10/10/rick-scott-wants-to-shift-university-funding-away-from-some-majors/

Aristotle. 1998. *The Nicomachean Ethics.* Trans. David Ross. Oxford: Oxford University Press.

Aron, Raymond. 1957. *The Opium of the Intellectuals.* New York: W.W. Norton & Company.

Aronowitz, Stanley. 1999. "The Unknown Herbert Marcuse." In *Social Text.* Vol. 17:1. Pp. 133–154.

Bacow, Lawrence S., William G. Bowen, Kevin M. Guthrie, Kelly A. Lack, and Matthew P. Long. "Barriers to Adoption of Online Learning Systems in U.S. Higher Education." *Ithaka S+R.* May 1, 2012.

Bailey, Holly. "Romney: Cabinet Won't Be Filled with 'Academics and Politicians.'" In *ABC News*. July 10, 2012. www.abcnews.go.com/Politics/OTUS/romney-cabinet-filled-ac...

Barthes, Roland. 1977. *Image – Music – Text*. Trans. Stephen Heath. New York: Hill and Wang.

Bender, Michael C. "Scott: Florida Doesn't Need More Anthropology Majors." In *The St. Petersburg Times*. October 10, 2011. www.tampabay.com/blogs/the-buzz-florida-politics/content/scott-florida-doesnt-need-more-anthropology-majors

Benjamin, Walter. "The Work of Art in the Age of Mechanical Reproduction." In *Illuminations*. Ed. Hannah Arendt. New York: Schocken Books.

Bingham, Amy. "Ron Paul's Economic Plan Eliminates Department of Education and Five Others." In *ABC News*. October 18, 2011. www.abcnews.go.com/blogs/politics/2011/10/ron-pauls-economic-plan-eliminates-department-of-education-and-5-others/

Bishop, Tana. "Research Highlights: Cost Effectiveness of Online Education." *The Sloan Consortium*. 2006.

Bloom, Allan. 1987. *The Closing of the American Mind*. New York: Simon & Schuster.

Bowen, William G. and Matthew M. Chingos, Kelly A. Lack, and Thomas I. Nygren. "Interactive Learning Online at Public Universities: Evidence from Randomized Trials." *Ithaka S+R*. May 22, 2012.

Bronner, Stephen Eric. 1994. *Of Critical Theory and Its Theorists*. Cambridge, Massachusetts: Blackwell Publishers.

Bronner, Stephen Eric. 2002. *Imagining the Possible*. New York: Routledge.

Bronner, Stephen Eric. 2011. *Critical Theory: A Very Short Introduction*. Oxford: Oxford University Press.

Bruni, Frank. "Questioning the Mission of College." In the *New York Times*. April 20, 2013.

Caputo, Marc, and Steve Bousquet. "Gov. Rick Scott Unveils Budget of Deep Cuts to Spending, Taxes." In *Tampa Bay Times*. February 8, 2011.

Carlson, Tucker. "Tucker for July 24." *NBC News*. July 26, 2007. www.nbcnews.com/id/19976269/

Clark, Lesley. "Marco Rubio Returns to the Classroom, Teaching 'Florida Politics' at FIU." In *The Miami Herald*. June 2, 2011.

Cohen, Patricia. "Professor is a Label that Leans to the Left." In the *New York Times*. January 18, 2010.

Colavecchio, Shannon. "Lawmakers Stress Need for Higher Ed but Warn of Cuts." *In Tampa Bay Times*. February 28, 2010. www.tampabay.com/news/lawmakers-stress-need-for-higher-ed-but-warn-of-cuts/1076083

Connors, Molly A. K. "Gingrich: Blame 'Snob Effect.'" In *Concord Monitor*. August 26, 2011.

Diogenes Laertius. 1901. *The Lives and Opinions of Eminent Philosophers*. Trans. C. D. Yonge. London: George Bell and Sons.

DiSalvo, David. "How Governor Rick Scott is Sabotaging Florida's Universities." In *Forbes*. April 23, 2012. www.forbes.com/sites/daviddisalvo/2012/04/23/how-governor-rick-scott-is-sabotaging-floridas-universities

Dougherty, Michael Brendan. "The Story Behind Ron Paul's Racist Newsletters." In *The Atlantic*. December 21, 2011.

Engels, Friedrich. 1978. "Socialism: Utopian and Scientific." In *The Marx-Engels Reader*. Ed. Robert Tucker. New York: W.W. Norton & Company.

Farr, Arnold L. 2009. *Critical Theory and Democratic Vision*. Lanham, Maryland: Lexington Books.

Ferretter, Luke. 2006. *Louis Althusser*. New York: Routledge.

Fish, Stanley. "Politics and the Classroom: One More Try." In the *New York Times*. June 8, 2008.

Flannery, Mary Ellen. "Study Shows Students Taking Online Courses More Likely to Fail." *NEAToday.org*. July 26, 2011.

Flechas, Joey. "UF May Get $15 Million Extra to Pursue Top 10 Status." In the *Gainesville Sun*. January 31, 2013.

Freud, Sigmund. 1961. *Civilization and Its Discontents*. Trans. James Strachey. New York: W.W. Norton & Company.

Freud, Sigmund. 1966. *Introductory Lectures on Psychoanalysis.* Trans. James Strachey. New York: W.W. Norton & Company.

Friedman, Thomas. "The Professors' Big Stage." In the *New York Times.* March 5, 2013.

Fry, John. 1974. *Marcuse—Dilemma and Liberation.* Sussex: The Harvester Press.

Fuchs, Stephan. 2001. *Against Essentialism: A Theory of Culture and Society.* Cambridge, Massachusetts: Harvard University Press.

Fuller, Andrea. "Iona College Admits Reporting of Falsified Data." In *The Chronicle of Higher Education..* November 8, 2011.

Gordon, Larry. "Claremont McKenna College Under Fire for SAT Cheating Scandal." In *Los Angeles Times.* January 31, 2012.

"Governor's Science, Technology, Engineering & Math Advisory Council." In *Mass.gov.* www.mass.gov/governor/administration/ltgov/lgcommittee/stem/

Green, Randiah. "College Republicans Compiling List of Liberal Professors at Ohio School." On Fox News. August 31, 2009.

Greimas, Algirdas Julien. 1979. "About Games." In *SubStance.* Vol. 8: 4. Pp. 31–35.

Greimas, Algirdas Julien. 1987. *On Meaning.* Trans. Paul J. Perron and Frank H. Collins. Minneapolis: University of Minnesota Press.

Grunberg, Isabelle. 1990. "Exploring the 'Myth of Hegemonic Stability." In *International Organization.* Vol. 44:4. Pp. 431–477.

Gunnell, John G. 1985. "Political Theory and Politics: The Case of Leo Strauss." In *Political Theory.* Vol. 13:3. Pp. 339–361.

Hall, Dee J., and Samara Kalk Derby. "Gov. Scott Walker Unveils Agenda for Wisconsin During Speech in California." In *Wisconsin State Journal.* November 19, 2012. host.madison.com/news/local/govt-and-politics/gov-scott-walker-unveils-agenda-for-wis-consin-during-speech-in/article_a35a1378-31ed-11e2-bb6c-0019bb2963f4.html

Harris II, William F. 1982. "Bonding Word and Polity: The Logic of American Constitutionalism." In the *American Political Science Review.* Vol. 76:1. Pp. 34–45.

Hobbes, Thomas. 1996. *Leviathan.* Ed. Richard Tuck. Cambridge: Cambridge University Press.

Horowitz, Michael G. "Portrait of the Marxist as an Old Trouper." In *Playboy.* September 1970.

Huszar, Tibor. 1976. "Changes in the Concept of Intellectuals." In *The Intelligentsia and the Intellectuals.* Ed. Aleksander Gella. London: Sage Publications. Pp. 79–110.

Jacobs, A. J. "Two Cheers for Web U!" In the *New York Times.* April 20, 2013.

Jaggars, Shanna Smith, and Di Xu. "Online Learning in the Virginia College System." *Community College Research Center.* www.ccrc.tc.columbia.edu. September 2010.

Jaggars, Shanna Smith, and Di Xu. "Online and Hybrid Course Enrollment and Performance in Washington State Community and Technical Colleges." *Community College Resource Center.* www.ccrc.tc.columbia.edu. March 2011.

Jameson, Frederic. 1981. *The Political Unconscious.* Ithaca: Cornell University Press.

Jameson, Frederic. 2005. *Archaeologies of the Future.* New York: Verso.

Jameson, Frederic. 2006. "First Impressions." In *London Review of Books.* Vol. 28:17. Pp. 7–8.

Jameson, Frederic. 2007. *Jameson on Jameson: Conversations on Cultural Marxism.* Ed. Ian Buchanan. Durham: Duke University Press.

Jaschik, Scott. "AAUP Survey Finds that Average Faculty Salary Increased by Rate of Inflation in Last Year." In *Inside Higher Ed.* April 8, 2013.

Jester, Erin. "Jesus-Stomping Incident at FAU Draws Rebuke from Rick Scott." In *The Miami Herald.* March 26, 2013.

Johnson, Paul. 1988. *Intellectuals.* New York: Harper & Row Publishers.

June, Audrey Williams and Jonah Newman. "Adjunct Project Reveals Wide Range in Pay." In *The Chronicle of Higher Education.* January 4, 2013.

Katz, Barry. 1982. *Herbert Marcuse and the Art of Liberation.* New York: Verso.

Kellner, Douglas. 1994. "A Marcuse Renaissance?" In *Marcuse: From the New Left to the Next Left.* Ed. John Bokina and Timothy J. Lukes. Lawrence, Kansas: University of Kansas Press.

Kellner, Douglas. 2004. "Marcuse and the Quest for Radical Subjectivity." In *Herbert Marcuse: A Critical Reader.* Ed. John Abromeit and Mark W. Cobb. New York: Routledge.

Kors, Alan Charles, and Harvey A. Silverglate. 1998. *The Shadow University.* New York: The Free Press.

Kowsar, Mohammad. 1983. "Althusser on Theatre." In Theatre Journal. Vol. 35:4. Pp. 461–474.

Laclau, Ernesto, and Chantal Mouffe. 2001. *Hegemony and Socialist Strategy.* New York: Verso.

Lenin, V. I. 1987. "What Is to Be Done?" In *Essential Works of Lenin.* Ed. Henry M. Christman. New York: Dover Publications.

Lilla, Mark. 2001. *The Reckless Mind: Intellectuals in Politics.* New York: New York Review of Books Press.

Lind, Peter. 1985. *Marcuse and Freedom.* New York: St. Martin's Press.

Lukacs, Georg. 1971. *History and Class Consciousness.* Trans. Rodney Livingstone. Cambridge, Massachusetts: MIT Press.

Lukes, Timothy J. "Mechanical Reproduction in the Age of Art: Marcuse and the Aesthetic Reduction of Technology." In *Marcuse: From the New Left to the Next Left.* Eds. John Bokina and Timothy J. Lukes. Lawrence, Kansas: University of Kansas Press.

Lutz, Byron, Raven Molloy, and Hui Shan. 2010. "The Housing Crisis and State and Local Government Tax Revenue." *Federal Reserve Board of Governors.* www.federalreserve.gov/pubs/feds/2010/201049/201049pap.pdf

MacIntyre, Alasdair. 1970. *Herbert Marcuse.* New York: The Viking Press.

MacIntrye, Alasdair. 1984. *After Virtue.* Notre Dame, Indiana: University of Notre Dame Press.

MacKey, Theresa M. 2001. "Herbert Marcuse." In *Dictionary of Literary Biography*, Volume 242. Ed. Paul Hansom. Los Angeles: The Gale Group. Recovered from www.marcuse.org/herbert/biog/Mackey2001.htm

Marcuse, Hebert. 1955. *Eros and Civilization.* Boston: Beacon Press.

Marcuse, Herbert. 1961. *Soviet Marxism.* New York: Vintage Books.

Marcuse, Herbert. 1964. *One-Dimensional Man.* Boston: Beacon Press.

Marcuse, Herbert. 1965. "Socialist Humanism?" In *Socialist Humanism.* Ed. Erich Fromm. New York: Doubleday.

Marcuse, Herbert. 1969. *An Essay on Liberation.* Boston: Beacon Press.

Marcuse, Herbert. 1970a. "Repressive Tolerance." In *A Critique of Pure Tolerance.* Eds. Robert Paul Wolff, Barrington Moore, Jr., and Herbert Marcuse. Boston: Beacon Press.

Marcuse, Herbert. 1970b. "The End of Utopia." In *Five Lectures.* Trans. Jeremy J. Shapiro and Shierry M. Weber. Boston: Beacon Press.

Marcuse, Herbert. 1972a. *Studies in Critical Philosophy.* Trans. Joris De Bres. Boston: Beacon Press.

Marcuse, Herbert. 1972b. *Counterrevolution and Revolt.* Boston: Beacon Press.

Marcuse, Herbert. 1978. *The Aesthetic Dimension.* Trans. Erica Sherover. Boston: Beacon Press.

Marcuse, Herbert. 1998. "Some Remarks on Aragon: Art and Politics in the Totalitarian Era." In *Technology, War and Fascism.* Ed. Douglas Kellner. New York: Routledge.

Markoff, John. "Online Education Venture Lures Cash Infusion and Deals with Five Top Universities." In *New York Times.* April 18, 2012.

Markoff, John. "California to Give Web Courses a Big Trial." In *New York Times.* January 15, 2013a.

Markoff, John. "Essay-Grading Software Offers Professors a Break." In *New York Times.* April 4, 2013.

Marks, Robert W. 1970. *The Meaning of Marcuse.* New York: Ballantine Books.

Martineau, Alain. 1986. *Herbert Marcuse's Utopia.* Montreal: Harvest House.

Marx, Karl. 1904. *A Contribution to the Critique of Political Economy.* Trans. N. I. Stone. Chicago: Charles H. Kerr & Company.

Marx, Karl. 1963. *The 18th Brumaire of Louis Bonaparte.* Trans. C. P. Dutt. New York: International Publishers.

Marx, Karl. 1976. *Capital, Volume I.* Trans. Ben Fowkes. London: Penguin Books.

Marx, Karl. 1978a. "Contribution to the Critique of Hegel's Philosophy of Right." In *The Marx-Engels Reader.* Ed. Robert C. Tucker. New York: W.W. Norton.

Marx, Karl. 1988. *Economic and Philosophic Manuscripts of 1844.* Trans. Martin Milligan. Buffalo, NY: Prometheus Books.

Marx, Karl. 1993. *Grundrisse.* Trans. Martin Nicolaus. London: Penguin Books.

Marx, Karl, and Friedrich Engels. 1985. *The Communist Manifesto.* Trans. A. J. P. Taylor. London: Penguin Books.

Marx, Karl, and Friedrich Engels. 1998. *The German Ideology.* Amherst, New York: Prometheus Books.

Mussolini, Benito, and Giovanni Gentile. 2011. "The Doctrine of Fascisim." In *Ideals and Ideologies.* Eds. Terence Ball and Richard Dagger. Boston: Longman.

Odland, Steve. "College Costs Out of Control." In *Forbes.* March 24, 2012.

Padgett, Tim. "Rick Scott's Tea-Friendly Budget Cuts: Too Deep?" In *Time.* February 14, 2011.

Palin, Sarah. 2010. *America By Heart.* New York: HarperCollins Publishers.

Parker, Kim, Amanda Lenhart, and Kathleen Moore. "The Digital Revolution and Higher Education: College Presidents, Public Differ on Value of Higher Learning." *Pew Internet & American Life Project.* August 28, 2011.

Parry, Marc. "Colleges See 17 Percent Increase in Online Enrollment." *Chronicle of Higher Education.* January 26, 2010.

Peoples, Steve. "Cain Meeting with Union Leader Newspaper Canceled." In *The Huffington Post.* November 17, 2011. www.huffingtonpost.com/huff-wires/20111117/us-cain/

Peralta, Eyder. "After Controversy, David Petraeus Will Now Earn $1 Teaching." On National Public Radio. July 16, 2013. www.npr.org

Pomerantz, Dylan. "10 Ways to Get Yourself Fired." In *The Chronicle of Higher Education.* April 25, 2012.

Portman, Rob. "Gay Couples Also Deserve Chance to Get Married." In *Columbus Dispatch.* March 15, 2013.

Republican Party of Texas. 2012. "Report of Platform Committee." www.texasgop.org/about-the-party

Riedweg, Christoph. 2005. *Pythagoras: His Life, Teaching, and Influence.* Ithaca: Cornell University Press.

Robinson, Peter. "Milton Friedman, Ronald Reagan and William F. Buckley Jr." In *Forbes.* December 12, 2008.

Rosenberg, Brian. "Ignorance About Education." In *Huffington Post.* January 30, 2013

Ruiz, Rebecca R. "Florida Governor Wants Funds to Go to Practical Degrees." In *New York Times.* October 13, 2011. www.thechoice.blogs.nytimes.com/2011/10/13/rick-scott/

Schleifer, Ronald. 1987. *A. J. Greimas and the Nature of Meaning: Linguistics, Semiotics and Discourse Theory.* Lincoln: University of Nebraska Press.

Scott, Rick. "Gov. Rick Scott: We Must Improve Education in Florida." In *The Gainesville Sun.* December 4, 2011. www.gainesville.com/article/20111204/OPINION03/111209931

Seidman, Steven. 1996. "The Political Unconscious of the Human Sciences." In *The Sociological Quarterly.* Vol. 37:4. Pp. 699-719.

Solochek, Jeff. "Rick Scott's Development Priorities Include Focus on STEM Education." In *Tampa Bay Times.* October 12, 2011. www.tampabay.com/blogs/gradebook/content/rick-scotts-economic-development-priorities-include-focus-stem-education

Sowell, Thomas. 2006. *Intellectuals and Society.* New York: Basic Books.

STEM Advisory Council. "A Foundation for the Future: Massachusetts' Plan for Excellence in STEM Education (Version 1.0). June 13, 2012. www.mass.gov/governor/administration/ltgov/lgcommittee/stem/ma-stem-plan.pdf

Steuernagel, Trudy. 1994. "Marcuse, the Women's Movement, and Women's Studies." In *Marcuse: From the New Left to the Next Left.* Ed. John Bokina and Timothy J. Lukes. Lawrence, Kansas: University of Kansas Press.

Stoekl, Allan. 2004. "Review of *The Reckless Mind: Intellectuals in Politics* by Mark Lilla." In *South Central Review.* Vol. 21:2. Pp. 89-93.

Strauss, Leo. 1952. *Persecution and the Art of Writing.* Chicago: University of Chicago Press.

Strauss, Leo. 1959. *What is Political Philosophy?* Chicago: University of Chicago Press

Strauss, Leo. 1964. *The City and Man.* Chicago: University of Chicago Press.

Suskind, Ron. "Faith, Certainty, and the Presidency of George W. Bush." In the *New York. Times.* October 17, 2004.

Travis, Scott. "College Tuition Should Vary By Degree, Florida State Task Force Says." In *Huffington Post.* October 25, 2012. www.huffingtonpost.com/2012/10/25/state-proposal-vary-cost_n_2014802.html

Turner, Jim. "Scott Wants Universities to Outline How Students will Help Florida Economy." In *Sunshine State News.* October 25, 2011. www.sunshinestatenews.com/story/rick-scott-wants-universities-outline-how-students-will-help-florida-economy

Turner, Jim. "Rick Scott Signs Law Creating State's 12th Public University for STEM Degrees." In *Sunshine State News.* April 20, 2012. www.sunshinestatenews.com/story/university-vital-creating-science-engineering-students-given-early-life-gov-rick-scott

Vennochi, Joan. "How Brown Lost Support from Women." In *The Boston Globe.* November 8, 2012.

Vivas, Eliseo. 1971. *Contra Marcuse.* New Rochelle, NY: Arlington House.

Waltz, Kenneth. 1979. *Theory of International Politics.* Reading, Massachusetts: Addison-Wesley Publishing.

Waever, Ole. 1990. Review of "The Language of Foreign Policy" by Walter Carlsnaes. In *Journal of Peace Research.* Vol. 27:3. Pp. 335-343.

Weber, Max. 1946. *From Max Weber.* Eds. H. H. Gerth and C. Wright Mills. Oxford: Oxford University Press.

Wegner, Phillip E. 2009. "Greimas Avec Lacan; or, From the Symbolic to the Real in Dialectical Criticism." In *Criticism.* Vol. 51:2. Pp. 211-245.

Weinstein, Adam. "Rick Scott to Liberal Arts Majors: Drop Dead." In *Mother Jones.* October 11, 2011.

Weisberg, Jacob. "What Caused the Economic Crisis?" In *Slate Magazine.* January 9, 2010. www.slate.com/articles/news_and_politics/the_big_idea/2010/01/what_caused_the_economic_crisis.html

Wilmath, Kim. "Gov. Rick Scott Signs $70 Billion State Budget After $142.7 Million in Vetoes." In *Tampa Bay Times.* April 18, 2012. www.tampabay.com/news/politics/gubernatorial/article1225440.ece

Wilmath, Kim. "Bill to Increase Tuition at UF, FSU Vetoed by Gov. Rick Scott." In *Tampa Bay Times.* April 27, 2012. www.miamiherald.com/2012/04/26/2772102/bill-to-increase-tuition-at-uf.html

Index

academic curriculum, 4, 6, 12, 14, 20, 27, 28, 29, 51, 97, 103
adjunct instructors, 84
Adorno, Theodor, 2, 4, 8, 97
alienation of reason, 47, 48, 51, 67, 92
Althusser, Louis, 1, 6, 8, 11, 12–13, 14, 15–17, 19, 21, 25–26, 29, 30n4, 52, 54, 55, 57, 58, 67, 69, 70, 71–72, 76, 79, 80, 81n2, 81n4, 93, 99, 101; Ideological State Apparatus, 6, 16–17, 19, 21, 56, 67, 101; interpellation, 16, 19, 21, 27, 63, 65, 66, 67, 70, 102; Repressive State Apparatus, 16, 17
Aristophanes, 32, 48
Aristotle, 81n2
Aron, Raymond, 7, 31, 34, 38, 39, 42

Barthes, Roland, 8
Benjamin, Walter, 4, 8, 41, 68–69, 81n6, 97; aura, 68
Bloom, Allan, 2, 3
Bonald, Louis, 22, 23
Bronner, Stephen Eric, 2, 3, 77, 100
Brown, Scott, 42, 44
Buckley, William F., 42, 49n10
Burke, Edmund, 22, 23

Cain, Herman, 42
City University of New York, 84
Claremont McKenna College, 58

class consciousness, 7, 15, 61, 62, 63, 64, 65, 67, 97
consumerism, 52, 54, 58, 60, 63, 64, 65, 66, 67, 97, 100
consumer capitalism, 52
consumer consciousness, 64, 65, 97
counterrevolution, 1, 3, 4, 5–6, 7–8, 13, 14, 22–26, 27, 28–29, 33–34, 38, 47, 48, 51, 52, 53, 54, 61, 64, 65, 66, 67, 69, 72, 76, 79, 80, 81, 83, 84, 86, 87, 92, 93, 95, 96, 97, 97–99, 100–101, 102, 103–104

David, Keith, 66
de Maistre, Joseph, 22, 23
Diogenes of Sinope, 104

Engels, Friedrich, 53, 54, 66n1, 88, 96
esotericism, 38
ExxonMobil, 60

false consciousness, 62, 63, 64, 66n6, 101
fascism, 28, 29, 97
Florida Atlantic University, 97
Florida International University, 59, 60, 84
Florida State University, 19
Florida Virtual School, 75
Frankfurt School, 2, 8
Freud, Sigmund, 89
Friedman, Thomas, 83, 85, 99

About the Author

Sean Noah Walsh is a lecturer of political theory in the Department of Politics & International Relations at Florida International University. He earned his doctorate in political science at the University of Florida in 2010. His research and teaching interests include Marxism and critical theory, ancient political thought, and Lacanian psychoanalysis. Walsh is also the author of *Perversion and the Art of Persecution* (Lexington Books 2012).